£2.99 ②
JuL

He

G000144133

Heart to Heart

**Eight ways to understand and heal
your vital connection to God**

Ali Martin and Liza Hoeksma

Authentic

Copyright © 2012

18 17 16 15 14 13 12   7 6 5 4 3 2 1

First published 2012 by Authentic Media Limited
52 Presley Way, Crownhill, Milton Keynes, MK8 0ES
www.authenticmedia.co.uk

The right of Ali Martin and Liza Hoeksma to be identified as the
Authors of this Work has been asserted by them in accordance with the
Copyright, Designs and Patents Act 1988

All rights reserved. No part of this publication may be reproduced, stored in
a retrieval system, or transmitted in any form or by any means, electronic,
mechanical, photocopying, recording or otherwise, without the prior
permission of the publisher or a licence permitting restricted copying.
In the UK such licences are issued by the Copyright Licensing Agency,
Saffron House, 6–10 Kirby Street, London, EC1N 8TS.

British Library Cataloguing in Publication Data
A catalogue record for this book is available from the British
Library
ISBN 978-1-85078-995-6

Unless otherwise stated Scripture quotations are taken from the
HOLY BIBLE, NEW INTERNATIONAL VERSION. Copyright © 1973, 1978,
1984 by Biblica. Used by permission of Hodder & Stoughton Publishers, a
member of the Hachette Livre UK Group. All rights reserved. 'NIV' is a
registered trademark of Biblica, UK trademarknumber 1448790.
Scripture taken from The Message. Copyright © 1993, 1994, 1995, 1996, 2000,
2001, 2002. Used by permission of NavPress Publishing Group.
Scripture quotations taken from the Amplified® Bible, Copyright © 1954,
1958, 1962, 1964, 1965, 1987 by The Lockman Foundation.
Used by permission. (www.Lockman.org)
Scripture taken from the HOLY BIBLE, TODAY'S NEW INTERNATIONAL
VERSION®. Copyright © 2001, 2005 by Biblica®. Used by permission of
Biblica®. All rights reserved worldwide.
Scripture quotations marked (NLT) are taken from the Holy Bible, New
Living Translation, copyright © 1996, 2004, 2007 by Tyndale House
Foundation. Used by permission of Tyndale House Publishers, Inc.,
Carol Stream, Illinois 60188. All rights reserved.

Cover design by David Smart
Printed and Bound by CPI Group (UK) Ltd., Croydon, CR0 4YY

For Richard and Prue who have helped heal countless hearts. We are truly privileged to have you in our lives.

Contents

Foreword

Heart to Heart is an amazing book of grace and truth. It is filled with great biblical teaching applied brilliantly to our lives. Someone once said we are human beings before we are human doings. This is a book that brings us back to the truth about who we are and who we were created to be. It helps us understand some of the events in our lives that may have prevented us from being fully human and fully alive, and leads us to the one who can overcome those obstacles and bring us back to fullness of life. Ali and Liza speak truth – truth that sets us free – into our hearts and minds, directly and clearly. They also speak grace as the truth is applied with compassion, understanding and sensitivity. They are both vulnerable and honest about their own stories and have included a number of other powerful testimonies that serve to strengthen, encourage and comfort. I love the way the stories themselves teach as well as wonderfully illustrating the scriptural teaching.

Who we are determines what we say and what we do. 'For out of the overflow of the heart the mouth speaks' (Matthew 12:34) so it is vital that our hearts are right. This book tells us how it is also possible and gives many insights into how we can put our hearts in the way of God's grace so this can happen.

I have known both Ali and Liza for over eighteen years as their Pastor, colleague and friend. I have watched with admiration and inspiration as they have worked the teaching in this book out in their own lives. *Heart to Heart* is not written from an ivory tower but is the overflow of two hearts and two lives that seek to follow their Saviour and let nothing get in the way of that pursuit.

I wholeheartedly recommend this book and its authors to you.

Mike Pilavachi
Soul Survivor
March 2012

1

Keeping Watch
(Ali)

Above all else, guard your heart, for it is the wellspring of life. (Proverbs 4:23)

They say you never forget your first love. That's true in my case, perhaps because my first love completely and utterly broke my heart. I was 17 years old and I met Phil when we were put together in a worship band for an event on a double-decker bus. Yep, it was 1992 and this was cutting edge. He was on piano and I was backing vocals, and when he got behind his piano and started to play it was love at first sight. For me, at least. We had to spend a number of evenings practising, during most of which I barely remembered to sing as I stared longingly and lovingly at him. On the day of the event I thought I was getting a little glimpse of heaven, singing next to the guy of my dreams. I didn't want to let the opportunity pass me by so, at the end of the day, I waited until he was alone and then I sidled up to him, to hit him with my best line. As it turned out, my best line was 'Great piano playing'; perhaps not all that brilliant. And then I left. I went home, lay on my bed and cried for the rest of the evening – convinced now the double-decker bus worship event was over I would never see him again. That was possibly a little dramatic seeing as he lived up the road from me, but then I've always been a bit of a drama queen.

I hoped and prayed God would bring us together again and, lo and behold, the next week I was at a friend's party and there he was – my dreamboat piano player. Not wanting to spend another afternoon crying on my bed I plucked up some courage and asked him out. Well, what I actually did was give him an 'I've never felt this way about anyone before' speech; it was a little full on but amazingly he was not put off by my slightly stalker-ish behaviour.

I will never forget our first date, nor the dates that followed. I'll never forget the first time he took my hand. I'll never forget our first kiss. And I'll certainly never forget the day he dumped me, because that was the day my heart broke in two. From that moment my world turned upside down. I was too distraught to go to school for days and even when my mum eventually got me to return, I was a wreck. I sat in my lessons with tears streaming down my face, which, now I think about it, must have been quite off-putting for my teachers. For weeks I cried and mourned and wore black. My family threatened to destroy my copy of Whitney Houston's 'I will always love you' which I played on repeat at top volume.

The pain showed no signs of abating and a few months into the agony our youth group went camping for the weekend. One of my leaders, Helen, came to chat to me about how I was doing and, without even asking my permission, she prayed a prayer over me that took me completely by surprise. She prayed, 'Lord, I ask that this break-up won't stop Ali from having a soft and vulnerable heart.' I was so mad! As far as I could tell it was having a soft and vulnerable heart that had got me into this mess; if my heart was harder, then it wouldn't be hurting quite so much. I *wanted* it to toughen up a bit so I wouldn't have to go through this kind of pain again. At the time, it felt like a mean prayer but I now know she prayed exactly the right thing. I might have wanted to harden my heart but God didn't want me to toughen up; he wanted my heart soft. Not because I'm a girl or because he liked seeing me in such pain. But because my heart – and your heart – are central to the way we respond to God. Our hearts are the very core of our beings. They are absolutely fundamental to how we see ourselves, others and God; how we feel about our past, what we do with our todays, and what we believe and hope for our tomorrows.

Our actions, attitude and behaviour are directly related to the state of our hearts. Luke 6:45 says the words we speak flow directly out of our hearts and in Romans 10:10 Paul reminds us it is with our hearts that we believe in and receive Jesus. When we become Christians we often pray that God would come into our hearts because we read in Ephesians 3:17 that Christ lives in our hearts through faith. When we surrender to him he comes and takes up residence in the centre of who we are. It's with our hearts we trust (Proverbs 3:5), it's with our hearts we feel and it's often with our hearts we make decisions. The state of our heart will determine how we live, how we act, how we pursue the life that God has for us. *Our heart is central to our response to God.*

It's no wonder then that the Bible calls us to keep a close and careful eye on the state of our hearts. In fact it says:

> Above all else, guard your heart, for it is the wellspring of life. (Proverbs 4:23)

We are to carefully and diligently guard our hearts above all else.

Let's pause on that first part for a second. 'Above all else' the writer says. More than anything else we do, more than anything else we think about and prioritise, we are to prioritise the state of our hearts. We are to carefully and diligently guard our hearts above all else. That's an incredible thing when you think about the implications. When I read that again recently I couldn't quite believe it. Can it really be true there is no higher priority than what is going on in our hearts? To understand why this is true, we need to grasp that our heart is absolutely essential to our response to God and how we live our lives for him.

If it is the most important thing, does that mean it is more important than *serving* God? Yes. Because unless our serving comes from a heart of love for him it becomes empty deeds that mean nothing. Isn't *worship* important? Yes, but our worship can only flow from hearts that have been captured by God. Isn't it important to *read our Bibles* and get to know God? Yes, but we go to his word not to educate ourselves about him but to know him with our whole hearts. Isn't it important to *tell our friends* who don't know Jesus about him? Yes, but if he hasn't first captivated our hearts why would we want to?

The rest of the verse from Proverbs explains exactly why it is so important to guard our hearts so passionately. We are told our hearts are the 'wellspring of life'. They are the very place from which our whole life originates and flows. We know this is true physically – that without our heart to pump our blood round the body we die, and we die quickly. The heart gives life to the body, and, in a spiritual sense, the heart gives life to every other part of us too.

Guarding our hearts

We need to be careful about how we interpret the concept of guarding our hearts. Most of us have been hurt at some point in our lives and we've been tempted to protect ourselves from feeling that pain again by putting a ten-foot wall up around our hearts. If we've been severely hurt we top that wall with razor wire and broken glass. We want to build a fortress no one can come near and nothing can break through but that's not what God is talking about. Guarding our hearts does not mean we are to become hard, cynical and suspicious, keeping everyone at arm's length.

When we're told by God to guard our hearts, what he means is that we're to keep watch over them. We should keep an eye on them in the same way a good security guard might protect a building, keeping fully alert and looking carefully so that nothing about our hearts escapes our attention. We need to be deliberately watchful of what's going on in the centre of who we are, in the place from where life flows.

As I mentioned, our outward behaviour is a sign of what is going on in our hearts so this is a good place to start when we're examining our hearts. If you're anything like me, you may find yourself reacting or feeling something strongly in a situation, and you're not sure why. Perhaps you explode with anger at the smallest provocation, but deep down you know that isn't actually the thing making you so angry. Perhaps someone makes a casual comment that leaves you feeling so criticised you can't shake it off for days. Maybe your feelings are hurt by the slightest thing or you become anxious and tense and can't get to the bottom of what's worrying you. You sulk or withdraw, while angry or bitter thoughts rage through your head. There can be so many emotions and reactions flying around all the time that often we're not sure where all those feelings come from.

Thankfully, we're not on our own when it comes to working out what's going on. Jesus came to reveal our hearts (Luke 2:35) and in his presence we find we don't have to dig about to discover the state of our hearts, he will gently show us through the Holy Spirit. We can pray, like King David did in Psalm 139:23, 'Search me, O God, and know my heart'. He will let us know where our behaviour has been out of line, where our attitudes are harsh and unloving, where we're looking to the wrong things to fulfil our needs, or where we are hurting and need his healing. He doesn't force any of this on us, he waits for us to ask. So, if we're serious about understanding our hearts, we need to choose to deliberately and honestly come before God. There's no great mystery to it; it's just being in his presence with everything on the table, not hiding or holding anything back. In his presence there is healing and restoration. It's about allowing him to meet with us and change us.

I love David's prayer in Psalm 51. He wrote it after he had committed murder and slept with someone else's wife. Painfully aware of his sin he says:

> Create in me a pure heart, O God,
> and renew a steadfast spirit within me.
> Do not cast me from your presence
> or take your Holy Spirit from me.
> Restore to me the joy of your salvation
> and grant me a willing spirit, to sustain me. (51:10–12)

What a cry from David's heart: create, renew, restore. David knows he has messed up. He needs God's presence and help, and he asks for it. Whatever the state of our hearts, in God's presence we too can ask him to create, renew and restore us. It's what God loves to do; it's who he is: so we can rest assured he wants to.

Whatever the state of our hearts, in God's presence we too can ask him to create, renew and restore us.

Whatever has gone wrong, whatever has hardened our hearts, however long we've been ignoring our hearts, all is not lost. We can all pray alongside David that God would create, renew and restore our hearts. We can all ask God to mend our broken hearts, to soften our hard hearts, and heal our hurting hearts. We can claim a promise of God found in Ezekiel that he will remove our heart of stone and give us the gift of a heart of flesh (36:26). That might not feel a safe or appealing idea to you. When we become practised in protecting ourselves we fear having a heart of flesh because that means we'll begin to feel again and may even get hurt again. However, the Bible urges us to trust in the Lord with all our hearts (Proverbs 3:5). Circumstances are unreliable but God is our firm foundation. We can trust in his goodness, his character and his unfailing love for us.

I used to pick at the spots on my face, and though it started as a small, bad habit it became quite addictive. It got to the point where I would spend half an hour in the bathroom, picking at my face until it was red and bleeding, eventually ending up crying on the bathroom floor. Thankfully, my mum was wise enough to know it wasn't really about my spots at all and she asked me to think about what was going on in my heart and mind when I wanted to pick my spots. As I did that, I began to realise I felt angry and frustrated about different situations in my life and was taking that out on my face. It was like a form of self-harm; my physical outlet for emotions I hadn't known how to express. Realising what was going on underneath stopped me from feeling like I had a hopeless habit I couldn't break. I started to bring the anger and frustration to God and ask him to help me deal with it in a healthier way.

Jenny

In the coming chapters we want to explore our hearts and try to understand what state they are in. We want to bring our hearts deliberately and purposefully before God, asking him to examine them and show us where he wants to heal and change us. We want to explore whether we're at peace or full of anxiety, whether we're full of faith or struggling to trust God, and whether our heart is being fed by God or hungry and looking in the wrong places. We want to be honest with God about whether our hearts are soft or hard, and whether we have hope or feel numb. Ultimately, we want to consider whether our hearts are fully surrendered to Jesus and are free in his presence.

No matter what state our hearts are in, we can come to him and ask him to 'create, renew and restore'. This is not something we do; it's what he does, by his Holy Spirit. As you read on you will see lots of suggestions as to how you can explore the state of your heart. When you come across these suggestions, don't fall into the trap of beating yourself up or thinking you now have to do a whole series of things. It's simply about being open to God doing whatever he wants in our lives and allowing him to reveal what's happening in our hearts; to soften us where he needs to and to satisfy us so we can live strong, firm and secure in Jesus, but be soft and vulnerable in our hearts.

There are times when I start to feel kind of numb. I stop caring about things I know I normally care about, I realise I'm not laughing at things that would normally make me giggle, and I don't even cry at things that are sad. When I realise what's going on, I know to check what's happening in my heart because those are outward signs to me that I've hardened up a bit.

Sarah

Jo's story

Ever since I became a Christian when I was thirteen, my favourite verse has been from Psalm 34: 'The LORD is close to the brokenhearted and saves those who are crushed in spirit' (v. 18). I wonder if even back then my heart was broken because I never felt comfortable with who I was. At a young age I was bouncy, expressive, fidgety, loud and talkative but I was always told to sit still and be quiet so I began to associate my character traits with bad behaviour. I didn't feel affirmed in any good qualities, and with a lot going on at home I didn't feel safe enough to be me. I was constantly worried too. I worried about what other people thought of me and I wanted to please people so much I would do whatever they wanted to make them happy, even if that meant I was miserable.

I didn't know who I was supposed to be and life felt like a constant fight to try and work it out. I was trying to be who my mum wanted me to be, who my dad wanted me to be, who my school friends wanted me to be. Everyone wanted something different and I didn't know what was 'right'. It felt like if I was happy and fun I was told off for being too noisy. If I stayed quiet I was told off for being sad and mopey. When I was too friendly my friends rejected me but if I was stand-offish, they would get annoyed, and ask what was wrong with me. I felt voiceless. It didn't feel like my thoughts or feelings were heard or my opinions mattered. So I retreated more and more into myself to try and be safe.

It didn't help that I didn't feel like I was good at anything. I had a really nice group of friends but they all did brilliantly in school, whereas I struggled. They seemed to get As without putting in much effort, and I would study for hours and get nowhere near that. One of the only things I enjoyed was running. I loved the freedom it gave me. I held school records for sprinting and would run for hours in the evening. I'd leave the house and just keep running, praying I would get lost and wouldn't have to go home because home felt like a place of confusion rather than a place of safety. But, of course, eventually, I would have to turn around and go back, so I started dancing in my room to give me that same feeling of freedom. My church let me have the keys to one of their rooms so I could have more space to dance. I used to literally throw myself around it, smashing into the walls, jumping off furniture. I got covered in splinters but I didn't care: it was the one time I wasn't defined or confined by anyone or anything else. I had no dance training at that point but I just loved moving and the feeling that I was alone with God, just me and him. Those were the moments where I felt free to express all the emotions and complex feelings I didn't know what to do with. I could cry or smile and not be told off or be asked to change. For those moments it was like knowing I was OK, that God liked me too and that life was alright. When I had to shut the door on that room it wasn't so easy.

My friends started getting boyfriends. It seemed like there was a constant stream of guys wanting their attention but no one was interested in me. I figured I just wasn't pretty enough. I knew I couldn't change my face (though I desperately wanted to) but I could change my body shape and wondered if then someone might find me attractive. So I started cutting down on what I ate, and having a small snack at lunch instead of a normal meal. But, whilst I wanted boys to notice me, I was also nervous around them. Everything I'd seen about boys on TV and in magazines made me think they were only interested in one thing; it seemed like they used girls for sex but didn't really care about them. Then I met a guy who liked me – Nick. I was attracted to him and we got on well but pretty soon he confirmed all my fears about men. He started pressuring me to do things that I didn't want to do and I was too naive and too scared of offending him to say no. The other Christian girls at school were talking about the stuff they got up to with their boyfriends so I figured it couldn't be that bad, even if it made me feel uncomfortable and ashamed.

At that point I started being very intentional about cutting back on what I ate. I had never really enjoyed food, perhaps because meal times were always difficult when I was growing up. Everyone was tense and uncomfortable with each other and my sister and I felt we weren't supposed to talk. I didn't feel safe and began to associate that with food. But eating less as a teenager was about much more than food. I was so ashamed of what was going on with Nick that I wanted to be invisible. I wanted to hide. Although I'd initially wanted to lose weight to attract male attention, I began to feel like if I got very thin, Nick just wouldn't want to touch me anymore.

Friends began heading off for university but I had no idea what I wanted to do. I started working in a pub and did a course so I could be a nanny. I felt lost; I didn't know where I was headed and was feeling lonely and isolated too. I cut back again on what I was eating, began running and cycling more and the weight began to fall off me. By this point I'd been losing weight for a couple of years and my body started to collapse; I wasn't having periods but I didn't notice or care. I had no idea what I looked like. I felt ugly and ashamed. All I knew was I hated myself, I hated my life and I hated existing. It was agony not knowing who I was, not believing I had a voice and feeling like I was being mistreated. I just wanted to disappear.

What you don't always hear about anorexia is how painful it is. You are always empty, always hungry, always cold, always dizzy. Your mind is constantly filled with internal arguments over whether you should or shouldn't eat something, so each mouthful of food becomes a mountain to climb. You can't find clothes to fit and have to shop in children's stores to find sizes small enough. Taking a bath is agony as your bones protrude so much that sitting in the tub hurts every part of you. Trying to function day to day is almost impossible as you feel vacant most of the time and can't concentrate on anything or anyone. Your heart is in constant turmoil and it's exhausting. It's a disease that traps you and makes you feel utterly alone. Some nights I would lie in bed wondering if I would actually wake up the next day; at times I was petrified about what I was doing to myself but I didn't know how to stop. I didn't know how else to control the pain I was in: starving myself felt like the only way to be in control. The long-term implications of what I was doing to myself didn't cross my mind; I had no idea that anorexia could lead to brittle bones, Irritable Bowel Syndrome, infertility, heart-failure and even death. My heart was broken and I was completely unable to express the pain inside. I used to bang my head against a glass door at home in anger, frustration and hurt. I felt so trapped in the illness and couldn't see a way out. What I was doing to myself was a massive cry for help that I couldn't vocalise in any other way.

I became so ill I ended up losing my job. I'd moved on from the pub to working at a children's nursery and they saw I wasn't eating enough to cope with the physical demands of my job. I was surviving on half a crumpet a day. Nick broke up with me because he couldn't handle seeing me so ill. Not long after, I found out he had started seeing another girl who I was friends with. I fell apart. If I felt like my heart was broken before, now it felt like it was smashed to pieces. My mum took me to the doctors and they referred me to a counsellor and a dietician to help sort out my eating. I was given an eating plan and had to agree 'safe' foods I felt able to eat. It was a huge battle because, although I knew I needed to put food in my body to be able to function, all the pain was still there in my heart. I had to start eating better before I could properly begin counselling as my brain didn't have enough food to work, so trying to talk about my compli- cated and internalised thoughts and feelings was too hard. Each meal was a battle and I was expected to go from surviving on almost nothing to eating three meals a day with snacks in between. Most days it would take me 45 minutes just to eat my breakfast. At times, it felt like my days revolved around having to eat and as soon as I'd finished one thing, it was time to eat the next thing. It was exhausting and I sometimes wished they would just take me into hospital and drip feed me so I wouldn't have to go through it. I was weighed each week at the hospital, and I would avoid looking at the scales as I couldn't bear to see the weight going back on, even in tiny amounts. It was so hard as I had been so used to hiding every part of me and was now compelled to have my privacy invaded by doctors.

A breakthrough came when I went to stay with two Christian women on the beautiful Cornish coastline who had experience working with girls with anorexia. Each morning, I would walk along the cliffs and talk to God. I began to talk to him about what I was doing to my body and started to say sorry. I let out my anger at situations that had happened in my life, the ways I had been hurt and the confusion I felt about who I was. One day I found an amazing church overlooking the sea and it felt like I was alone with God. I stood on the edge of the cliff and screamed and yelled; it was so good to be vocalising my anger and pain. Those walks helped me reconnect with my own heart. I'd been blocking it out because I couldn't deal with it, and I'd spent so many years feeling as though no one accepted me and I hadn't accepted myself at all. That week, my heart and my body were fed. As I came back each day and talked with the two women I felt more and more accepted. The more accepted I felt, the easier it was to eat and I found myself taking a second piece of bread at lunch, or having ice cream at dinner, without the usual battle I'd had to face when it came to food. I began to laugh again. I could even smile at myself in the mirror rather than grimace and I could thank God for making me rather than praying he would take me away. I went home with hope my heart and my body could be healed.

It's been a long journey to recovery and it has taken many years. I've taken anti-depressants, seen plenty of dieticians and eating disorder specialists, spent years in counselling, had hours of prayer and cried my heart out a hundred times in worship. I don't have a great attention span and sometimes find reading the Bible tricky but worship has been a real place of healing for me. Sometimes, when we're lost in that place of love and adoration, God sneaks up and does something amazing in our hearts. I still felt like my heart was shattered but in worship it was easier to remember God had all the pieces in his hands. God has affirmed me in incredible ways, telling me who he made me to be and healing the pain in my heart from the lack of affirmation I had when I was growing up. I've also made amazing friends who believe in me and encourage me to be myself. I remember one evening I was at a party and, whilst it was winding down and people were clearing up, music was still playing. There was a wide open space so I just began to dance and dance. I was waiting for someone to laugh or tell me I wasn't being appropriate. Instead, they just delighted in who I was: that was freedom to me – to have friends who know who you are and enjoy it.

My pastors were an amazing support and even let me live with them for a year so they could help me. I had a mentor who would meet up with me each week and pray with me. I knew she loved me, believed in me and was completely trustworthy so I could be honest with her, but she wouldn't let me get away with anything. She told me I had to keep eating if we were to keep meeting together and that was a huge incentive.

There were setbacks along the way and it was by no means a smooth journey. Another turning point was when I was asked to dance at a worship event abroad. I was hugely excited as it was something I was so passionate about and it was a privilege to be asked. However, I wasn't eating properly, I had neither energy nor strength and the trip would include long days and irregular meal times which I knew wouldn't be good for me. It got to crunch time and I realised I was still too unwell to go. That was the first time I got angry with my illness. I was in my mid-twenties and I realised it was stealing my life and stopping me from doing things I loved. That summer I went to a Christian festival and, in one of the main meetings, the leader asked people to come forward who had eating disorders so they could be prayed for. Taking that step to get prayer was scary but it was a declaration before God and my friends that I wanted to get better. My friends gathered round to pray for me and one of them began to sing quietly in my ear; it was beautiful and felt like God was pouring out his healing and digging up the root of this ugly disease. I sobbed and sobbed, curled up in a ball on the floor and felt like I'd spiritually thrown up the root of this disease. When I looked up a good friend was sitting beside me. I said to her, 'It's gone!' and we both cried together at the wonderful thing God had done. The next day I ate a Cornish pasty which I'd remembered loving as a child but had not had for years. I ate every part of it without guilt or shame, then went and had tea too! I went to bed that night feeling like I was no longer consumed by my illness. I felt like I had space inside me – the pain had gone and there was finally room inside me for me to be me.

It's still been hard work since then but I feel like I'm finally getting my life back. God has restored relation-ships in amazing ways, and now eating a meal with my family is a lovely event. I find counselling extremely helpful as I never want to go back to that dark and awful place I was in. What I've learnt is that God is the rest-orer of hearts and minds. He is the great healer. When I was unwell life felt dark, painful and confusing and the anorexia was all consuming. I couldn't see any way out but God made a way: 'He brought me out into a spa-cious place; he rescued me because he delighted in me' (Psalms 18:19). I am enjoying learning more and more who God has made me to be and growing in that every day. I know God delights in me and believe he has spo-ken these words to me:

My beloved spoke and said to me,
'Arise, my darling,
my beautiful one, come with me.
See! The winter is past;
the rains are over and gone.
Flowers appear on the earth;
the season of singing has come'.
(Song of Songs 2:10–12a, TNIV)

2

The Trusting Heart
(Liza)

'Do not let your hearts be troubled.
Trust in God; trust also in me.' (John 14:1)

Trust is something we all exercise all day every day, but most of the time we don't even think about it. We trust that if we've set an alarm, it will go off in the morning and wake us up. We trust that if we do a job, we'll get paid at the end of the week or month. We trust that if the pizza box says it cooks in 14 minutes, it will cook in 14 minutes. All these tiny choices, and hundreds like them we make all the time, all require an element of trust.

When we're born we have no choice but to trust ourselves entirely into the care of others. Babies can't do anything for themselves: they can't even communicate what they want or need properly so they have to rely on their parents or carers to work it out. But, somewhere along the way trust gets broken and our hearts get hurt. It may be small things like believing you'd get a certain gift you wanted for your birthday and being disappointed when you received something else, or it might be something huge like a parent's abusive behaviour

Trust can seem like a
foolish option that
only leaves our hearts
open to hurt and
disappointment.

that breaks your trust. The
older we get, often the
more reasons we can find
not to trust people.
Because they are human
beings, even people who
love us will let us down.
Our parents make mis-
takes, our friends hurt
us, boyfriends break our
hearts. Trust can seem like
a foolish option that only
leaves our hearts open to
hurt and disappointment.'

The trouble is, we carry this lack of trust into our relationship with God who is worthy of our trust. If one of
our parents left us we may struggle to believe God will
never abandon us. If we've been punished for mistakes
we've made, we may find it hard to trust that because of
Jesus we are forgiven. If friends have betrayed us we
may wonder if God truly does have our best intentions
at heart. If we've been rejected by people or made to feel
inferior, we'll struggle to believe God loves us just as we
are. Whatever our problems with trust, we have to be
careful we don't transfer them onto God because this
can badly damage our relationship with him.

Trust in relationships

You don't have to be an expert to know good relationships are built on trust. If you don't trust someone to be
honest with you, you won't ask for their opinion. If you
don't trust them to give you good advice, you won't ask
for it. If you don't trust someone to love you for who you

are, you'll never relax long enough to have fun with them. The less you trust someone, the less grounds there is for you to talk, spend time together and deepen a relationship.

Of course, the same is true for our relationship with God. For it to function at its best, not just limping along but actually going places, we have to trust in him with all our hearts. If we put our faith and our trust in him life can be an amazing adventure. Noah had to spend a long time building an ark on dry ground before he got to see God did mean what he said. Joseph had to trust God had a plan for his restoration when he languished in jail for something he didn't do. Jesus had to trust his Father that the cross was the only way to restore our relationship with our maker. None of these acts of faith would have been possible without trust. We want to do things for God, don't we? We want to see him do great things in our lives and in the lives of those around us, which means that in our hearts we have to be willing to put our trust in God.

Sometimes, we want to stay in control of our lives, live how we want and stay in our comfort zone. It can sound a lot easier than taking risks, can't it? But that means we're trusting in ourselves and in our own abilities to get things done. God knows far better than us how life should be lived (he was the one who designed it, after all). If we live it our way, we'll probably make it through, often with some highs along the way, but will we truly have lived up to our potential? Doing it ourselves won't get our names listed with the men and women of faith who trusted God, took the risks he asked of them and saw him do astounding things because of it. Putting our trust in God may seem like a risk, it may be scary, but it will be an adventure and there is no safer place to be.

A few years ago I was asked if I would be interested in applying for a temporary job with an organisation whose vision and values I love a lot. Taking the job meant a move to England from Northern Ireland, but I felt a God hunch to go and to trust him, not knowing what it would lead to. I came across a story about Mother Theresa who, when asked how she always seemed to have so much clarity, responded by saying, 'What I have never had is clarity, and what I have always had is trust.' So I decided to trust the God hunch and I have been in England ever since, having had some great God adventures along the way, the best of which has been meeting and marrying one of the best human beings I have ever known!

Sarah

Trusting in God

So if we want to trust in God more, do we just make up our minds and do it, or are there some more practical things we can do? The psalmist says:

> Those who know your name will trust in you,
> for you, LORD, have never forsaken those who seek you.
> (Psalms 9:10)

This is a great place for us to start when we're looking at trust: the more we know who God is the better able we will be to trust him. The Bible shows us many characteristics of God and some are actually used as God's names. For example, in Genesis 22:13–14 (NLT) God is called 'Yahweh-Yireh' meaning 'The Lord will provide'. Abraham had seen God's provision to such an extent that he called him by that name. Hagar (the servant to Abraham's wife Sarah) called the Lord, 'The one who sees' (Genesis 16:13) because he spoke so intimately to her about her situation.

We see examples of all sorts of other characteristics of who God is throughout the Bible. We see he is our Saviour, Healer, and Friend, as well as a faithful God, a passionate God, and a loving God. The amazing thing is that God will never change. He is the same yesterday, today and forever (Hebrews 13:8), so we can trust from the God of the Bible, and the God we have seen in our own lives, that he will always be the same.

The Bible is our greatest source when it comes to understanding God's character and knowing who he is. The more we read it, study it and comprehend it, the more we will be able to trust that God is who he says he is. As we put our trust in him and follow him, we will see examples of his character in our own lives too.

Because I am self-employed I don't have a secure income and can never tell how much money I will get paid at the end of the month. It's a challenge for me to trust God but he has proved himself faithful time and time again. I can tell when I am not fully trusting in him to provide for me financially as I start doing my sums. Not your regular, keep-on-top-of-things sums, but avidly checking and re-checking what money I think I have coming in and whether that will cover my outgoings. When I start to do it compulsively I have to stop and ask God to help me to trust in him as my provider and not in my bank balance.

Becky

Our own 'understanding'

When it comes to trusting God, one of the verses that has helped me the most is this:

> Trust in the LORD with all your heart
> and lean not on your own understanding (Proverbs 3:5)

I'll admit something to you – at school I was a bit of a maths geek. Oh yes. I couldn't get enough of equations because I loved the logical process you went through to find the right answer and I loved that at the end there was an answer – you could find out exactly what x was and even re-do the equation with your answer to check you were right. I'd love it if life looked a bit more like that; put in the time and you come away with something clear and logical. But we all know it doesn't work like that, don't we? Each one of us has had things in our lives that just don't make sense. Some of them might be more understandable with the benefit of hindsight, others may stay a mystery until the day we die.

Most of the time I, and I think probably many of us, look at the world through our own eyes, or do what the psalmist referred to as 'leaning on our own understanding'. We look at the world and it doesn't make sense. Things go wrong, or just don't work out the way we thought they would, and we wonder if we can truly trust God. But, this verse tells us not to try and work it out for ourselves but to know God's wisdom is greater than our wisdom. He has the bigger picture and, rather than us trying to make sense of how the universe works based on our incredibly limited understanding, he wants us to look to him and trust in him.

If God asks us to do something that feels like a risk and we weigh it up from a rational, natural perspective, it can go something a little like this. God asks us to give a portion of our income away as a tithe. We think, 'But if I do that then how am I going to pay for the things I need? What if I don't have enough money left over for me?' So we conclude, 'I just don't have enough to give money away, maybe I'll do that when I'm older/richer/more secure.' If that's the case, then we just missed out on a whole lot of good stuff. We missed out on being obedient to God, on blessing other people and on the freedom that comes from trusting God enough to take care of our own needs as we do what he asks of us.

Of course, it's not just money we're talking about (although, strangely, that can be an area where many of us struggle to trust God). We have to trust God with other things too: our heart, our reputation, our relationships, our hopes and dreams, our health, our careers . . . the list goes on. So what does it look like to trust in God?

Whenever I'm in a situation where I need to trust God even though circumstances look a bit crazy, I always come back to this verse: '"For my thoughts are not your thoughts, neither are your ways my ways," declares the LORD. "As the heavens are higher than the earth, so are my ways higher than your ways and my thoughts than your thoughts."' (Isaiah 55:8-9). God does things completely differently to how we might, but that's because he knows so much more than we ever could!

Lea

Consequences of trust

God calls all of us to put our trust in him rather than in financial security, friendships, relationships, our gifts and abilities, our careers, our families – and anything else we're tempted to trust in. Yet how we act out our trust in God is going to vary from situation to situation, and from person to person.

I can have a tendency towards being a bit of a control freak and it's something God has been working on in me for many years now. I am a 'do-er' as well – show me a problem and I'll try and work out the solution (remember my love of maths?!). That means that often for me, to show I trust God, I have to stop and let him do something for me rather than trying to sort it out myself. That's not an everyday command (I'm not saying 'I trust God to get me dressed in the morning and I'm not putting on even a pair of socks myself!') but in particular situations, that's how I am asked to demonstrate my trust in my loving heavenly Father.

When God promised Abraham and Sarai that they would have a son, they had a difficult time trusting him because they were both old and well past child-bearing years. Their solution was to use Sarai's maidservant to produce an heir (see Genesis 16) which caused nothing but problems. Although the situation looked bleak from an earthly point of view (again, when looked at from 'our understanding'),

Sometimes, we need to show our trust by the steps we're prepared to take to follow God's command.

God didn't need any help giving Abraham a son and he did just as he had promised.

Sometimes, we need to show our trust by the steps we're prepared to take to follow God's command. Unsurprisingly, it's Noah who springs to mind here. I'm always amazed the ark got built, aren't you? Most of us would have spent years questioning whether we'd actually heard God correctly and whether there could be any reason to build an ark on dry land. Or worrying about what our friends and neighbours would say when they saw what we were doing. But, Noah got on with it, and when the rain came, he and his family were glad he did. Noah trusted God and did what he was asked to do so, for him, trust looked a lot like measuring out planks of wood and banging them together (OK, it was more technical than that, but you get the point).

Questions

Does trusting God mean we don't ask questions? In short – no! The psalmists in particular questioned God, pouring out their hearts to him, telling him about their frustrations and confusions. Take a look and see how many times the phrase 'yet I will trust in you' appears. It's as if the writer has a rant about the situation but then says, 'No matter how it looks, I still know you are good and true.' This is a fantastic model for us. God wants to have a genuine relationship with us, not one where we pretend everything is OK and only show him our shiny happy side. We need to be real in the way we come to God: we can be honest about our struggles and our pain, but ultimately, like the psalmist, we have to say, 'But you are God and you know best.'

Will I get what I want?

Sometimes, we're tempted to think if we trust in God everything will work out the way we want – because we're always looking for that magic formula, aren't we? The one that will make life easier for ourselves and those we love, the one that offers the key to a lifetime of happiness. Some preachers will tell you if you just believe enough you can have anything you want, but I don't think that's true. You don't see life going swimmingly for every person in the Bible who followed God, so why should we always expect an easy ride just because we're Christians? God calls us to trust in who he is because his character never changes, whereas there are many different reasons why circumstances may change and life not turn out the way we want.

One of our greatest examples of this type of trust is in the book of Daniel. When King Nebuchadnezzar demands that everyone should bow down to his gold statue or face certain death, three people refuse. Shadrach, Meshach and Abednego were having none of it and found themselves threatened by the king: bow down and worship or be thrown in the fire. It's a horrifying situation but their response is incredible and such a lesson for us:

> 'O Nebuchadnezzar, we do not need to defend ourselves before you in this matter. If we are thrown into the blazing furnace, the God we serve is able to save us from it, and he will rescue us from your hand, O king. But even if he does not, we want you to know, O king, that we will not serve your gods or worship the image of gold you have set up.' (Daniel 3:16–18)

Wow. They're not saying, 'OK God, let's do a deal: we won't bow down to the gold if you will save us.' They're saying to the person who is threatening their lives 'We know our God can save us, but if for whatever reason he chooses not to, it doesn't matter – he's still the only one who we will worship.' This is such an important lesson for us – we don't worship God because of what he can do for us but for who he is, regardless of what life throws at us. Similarly, we don't trust God because of what we see going on, we trust him because he told us he is trustworthy (John 14:1).

If we have hearts that trust God, we will:

- Be peaceful because we know God is taking care of us as we look to him.
- Have no fear of the future – whatever it brings we know God is with us and he is good.
- Know God loves us, and we will rest in that love, no matter what our circumstances are, knowing God has only the best intentions for us.
- Have the confidence to step out in the gifts God has given us.
- Believe God is the God of the Bible – the one who can do more than we can ever dream or imagine (Ephesians 3:20).

My story

A few years ago, God challenged me to trust him. To me, what he was asking seemed huge. He wanted me to leave my job in Public Relations without another job to go to. All I had was the dream I could be a writer. If I 'leant on my own understanding' this didn't make any sense at all. I had a mortgage to pay, I had very little experience in creative writing and no contacts or opportunities for any paid work. However, after I'd spent a long time praying about it, getting wisdom and advice from trusted friends and having more than a few 'couldn't be more relevant' sermons preached at me, I decided this was God. I knew I had to trust him and take the risk. Thankfully, when I left my job I was given a chunk of redundancy pay which made the financial risk seem a lot less, but what I hadn't bargained for was the risk to my reputation. My family (who aren't Christians) all thought I was crazy to leave a secure job to follow a dream. And it was so much harder than I'd thought when I met someone new and they asked what I did. It's a normal question but one I began to dread. What was I? I couldn't class myself as a writer when no one was paying me to write but I didn't want to say I was unemployed and have people think I was lazing about. Tricky. But nowhere near as tricky as when the redundancy money started to run out. I'd done what I felt God had asked and I'd written a book but I couldn't find anyone to publish it. I didn't know what to do with myself – was God going to come through or was he going to leave me stranded? When I looked at it logically – again through the eyes of 'my understanding' – it just didn't make sense. I thought I was going mad – desperate for God to speak and to help me see what was going on. I ended up having to take some temping work: my pride took a beating every day as I was treated like a brainless dogsbody.

Of course, throughout this time, God and I had many discussions about the situation. One time in church, I was sitting on the floor between a row of chairs, again speaking to God about how painful I was finding the situation and he said to me, 'What do you want?' My first response, if I am honest, was, 'Are you kidding me?! Haven't I told you about a thousand times each day about this dream I want to follow?' But I got over myself, decided to trust that if God was asking me again there must be a reason for it, so I said 'I want to write.' At that moment my pastor came over and asked me (while my eyes were still shut and I was still sat on the floor) if I would write a book with him. That was the start of a steady stream of writing work coming my way by God's hand. It has required me to live by faith as God has asked me to trust him to provide the work rather than to go out looking for it myself. But I cannot even begin to describe the blessing it is to see him provide again and again in the most amazing and unusual ways.

I could have said no to God right at the start. I could have stuck with an OK job just to play it safe. Instead, because I trusted God, he has opened up a whole new life to me, he's developed gifts I didn't even know I had, and I've had the joy and the privilege of seeing him working in my life in so many ways. I'm not going to pretend I've got the whole trust thing sewn up though (much as I'd like to). Sometimes I think of trust as a little bit like a high jump. God gives us plenty of opportunities to trust in him; when we take one and see he is worthy of that trust we have made that particular jump and next time we will be ready to jump a little higher. I still feel like there are huge areas of my life where I need to trust God and some days I manage it, some days I don't. Some days my heart is filled with all the good things God has done and all the things I know to be true of his character. Some days my heart is distracted by my own failings and weaknesses and I fall flat on my face. One thing I know every day though: I used to be a play-it-safe kind of person but now I've seen what God can do when I trust him, I know he is the safest risk of all and I wouldn't give up this adventure with him for anything.

3

The Peaceful Heart
(Ali)

A heart at peace gives life to the body
(Proverbs 14:30a)

There seems so much to get anxious about these days. There's the important issues like our health, exams, career, relationships and future. And the trivial everyday worries: does my hair look OK in this style? Am I getting a cold? Will my friend be offended I didn't text her back for a couple of days? Is it going to rain when I haven't got an umbrella?

If misery loves company then worry is the single biggest extrovert I know. Worry never likes to be alone – he always brings his mates and the 'what ifs' that trample through our minds can start to spiral out of control. Daily life is riddled with things to worry about but the

If misery loves company then worry is the single biggest extrovert I know.

Bible talks a lot about us having peace. In fact, Jesus said:

> 'Peace I leave with you; my peace I give you. I do not give to you as the world gives. Do not let your hearts be troubled and do not be afraid.' (John 14:27)

Paul takes this teaching seriously and passes it on to the Philippians in the form of a command:

> Do not be anxious about anything, but in everything, by prayer and petition, with thanksgiving, present your requests to God. And the peace of God, which transcends all understanding, will guard your hearts and your minds in Christ Jesus. (Philippians 4:6–7)

Here Paul is giving the Philippians and us a direct order not to be anxious. He's not gently letting us know God doesn't want us to worry, suggesting we try not to and adding 'but if you can't manage it, that's fine'. He's telling us that worry is not from God and it's not something we should be wasting our time and energy on. He's telling us this in the middle of a happy and joyful letter, not a cross one, so we should remember that like all of God's commands, this one is given to us for our own good. God's not trying to ruin our fun: he knows worry isn't good for us and won't give us life 'to the full' as he has promised (John 10:10).

Paul clarifies his point a step further: don't be anxious about anything, he says. Nothing! We can get stressed out, wound up, in a flap and freaked out about so many things but Paul says we're not to get worried about any of it.

So it sounds great, doesn't it? We'd all love to be free of anxiety, but how? Paul says it's by bringing everything to

God in 'prayer and petition'. In other words, as clichéd as it sounds, instead of worrying we need to pray. If we try and suppress things and stop worrying through our own power we'll simply squash the issue without dealing with it, or worry about the fact we're still worrying. When we pray instead we're choosing to bring the problem to our Father who we believe cares about what's going on in our lives and in our world. We choose to place the problem, however big or small, in his hands, rather than holding on to it ourselves. And the passage speaks of us continuing in prayer and petition. This means we need to keep on bringing it to God, handing our worries over again and again until we see him intervene in the situation. It's tempting to pray once, then continue worrying or trying to sort things out in our own strength, but when we keep handing things over and wait for God, we develop patience and trust, and it teaches us to persevere.

Sometimes, we can fall into the trap of thinking there are only certain things God wants us to talk to him about. The biggies are OK: we know we can pray for healing, for someone to become a Christian or for direction in our study and work. Often, it's the smaller things we let build up and bug us. We may think God isn't going to be interested in that conversation we had with a friend that's left us worrying about the relationship or the fact we feel like we're getting a cold. Yet Paul tells us to bring everything before God in prayer, and let's state the obvious: everything means everything! The big, the small, the in-between. God knows that most of us get worn down by the seemingly little things; they can stop us having life in all its fullness. The things I find myself worrying about are usually completely insignificant but they can still get my heart rate going and my stress level rising. It's amazing but God really doesn't see anything as being too small for him to be interested in. If it's of concern to us, then it's of concern to him. There isn't anything that he doesn't want to hear about because all things sit inside his love and care.

I, for one, am quite terrible at this. I'm good at the quick-fix prayers but terrible at waiting (and trusting) for God's intervention. When I was getting married, my husband-to-be, Joel, and I were looking for a flat to live in. We found the perfect place and fell in love with it, we prayed and asked God if we could live there. The first offer we made was low, and naturally was turned down, but instead of waiting on God like Joel would have had me do, I rushed in and offered the full asking price. I was so anxious we would miss out I did what I could to make the flat ours. It was only after the event I prayed about it, and realised we probably could have saved ourselves quite a bit of money if I had turned my worries into prayers and waited on God, instead of acting in my own strength.

The anxiety said something about what was going on in my heart. As I prayed about it I became aware my worries were coming from a mistaken belief that God didn't want to give me good things, and if I wanted something, I had to make it happen myself. I wasn't consciously working out of this belief but my reactions showed what was going on at the core of me. As I brought the situation to God, he revealed my heart and helped me bring the true problem before him, which was my understanding of his character. So often the things that cause us anxiety say more about what's going on behind the scenes than the actual situation. Whatever we're worrying about, we need to ask God to show us what is going on in our hearts keeping us from his peace. In every situation, he can bring us his comfort and wisdom.

Jesus talked about this link between understanding who God is and having peace. In Matthew 6 he tells us not to worry because we have a God who loves us, cares for us, knows what we need, and is more than capable of fulfilling those needs. God wants us to live in peace, knowing he is our provider. He also wants us to let go of our own agenda and submit ourselves to his will. He wants us to 'seek first his kingdom and his righteousness' over and above our own desires. And that's one of the reasons we pray. It's not always going to be about getting a 'yes' answer to what we want but praying helps us submit ourselves to God in order to find his peace. The same was true for Jesus. Think about the garden of Gethsemane on the night of Jesus' arrest. He was deeply distressed and overwhelmed with sorrow, so he prayed to his Father. At the end of his prayers the outcome hadn't changed and the cross still loomed before him but that didn't make the prayer meaningless. Jesus hadn't gone to the Father just to get a change of events; he'd gone to him because he was troubled and upset. He needed to submit himself to God's will again and to receive his strength and comfort for what lay ahead. If Jesus needed to do this then you can be sure we do too! We have to keep in mind that prayer always makes a difference even if it's not the difference we were hoping for or expecting. Sometimes we want to see change but God gives us peace and grace to handle things as they are.

I used to get really worried my church leaders would ask me to speak on a Sunday as they had asked lots of my friends. The very thought of it made me feel sick. I was anxious because I didn't have any confidence to speak in front of a large group of people and I was scared that if God asked me I couldn't say no and let him down. Eventually,

I asked a friend to pray with me about it. God showed me what my real fear was: I was scared that if I wasn't asked to speak, it was because I didn't have anything valuable to offer. God made me realise the real issue was about my identity in him and that I needed to know who he said I was. That gave me so much peace I stopped worrying about whether I got asked to speak or not!

Mary

Before I started a gap year course, I tried to raise as much money as I could to fund it but, as it got closer, I knew I wouldn't have enough to live on during the year. I was heartbroken! But instead of letting me panic I'd have to pull out, God reassured me he would provide. He told me he wanted me on the course and he was greater than any obstacle. As nice as words of affirmation from God are though, they don't always help me. I often still freak out but this time I wanted it to be different. I knew I couldn't deal with the problem myself so I gave it to God and the difference has been incredible. It doesn't bother me that I don't have the money already saved for food each week and that I don't know when I will next have money. When doubts ever creep into my mind, I can bat them away so easily because I just know – really know – that God will provide and I'll be fine!

Lahna

Giving thanks

Going back to the verse in Philippians 4, Paul gives us another key to having peaceful hearts. We're told to bring our requests in prayer with thanksgiving. This sounds like a bit of a curve ball here; we're talking about stress and anxiety and bringing this stuff to God when suddenly the notion of being thankful is thrown at us. But, actually, this is absolutely vital! In fact, the preceding verses say, 'Rejoice in the Lord always. I will say it again: Rejoice!' We must rejoice in God in all situations and this must include when we're stressed and anxious. Rejoicing lifts our eyes off the problem and onto our God who is bigger than any problem. It takes our focus away from the boulder in our path and onto the one who can move that boulder. Worry leads to worry; but worship leads to rejoicing. We should fix our eyes on Jesus and rejoice in him.

As we bring our requests, with thanksgiving, to our powerful and loving God, the promise follows that we will have the peace of God. Though we may not have our every wish fulfilled we will find that our hearts are at peace. Not the kind of peace that changes with circumstances or is dependent on what happens but the kind of peace Jesus showed when he was asleep on a boat in the middle of a storm. The wind would have been howling and the waves crashing around him (which is not ideal if you're in a boat) but Jesus didn't lose any sleep over it.

Though we may not have our every wish fulfilled we will find that our hearts are at peace.

That's the kind of peace I want. That's the kind of peace that Jesus and Paul were talking about. Nowhere in the Bible are we promised a life free from painful and difficult situations but we are promised peace despite our circumstances. I want to be someone who sleeps calmly while the boat is being battered around on the wind and waves of life. It's a peace that isn't dependent on things going our way, on getting the right grades or the right promotion. It's a peace that has no care for how much money is in the bank or what medical symptoms we're showing. It's a peace that transcends all understanding. A peace that doesn't make sense to the outside world but makes every sense to those of us who know God loves us and cares for us. It's a peace that comes from trusting God implicitly because when we think we're supposed to be in charge we can't help but panic and create a mess. When we leave it to God we know we're in the safest of hands.

We just need to remember to not get worked up and stressed about anything, anything at all! But in absolutely everything we do, without exception, let's keep on bringing the things concerning us to God. And let's do it with worship and thankfulness in our hearts, remembering God is able, powerful and loving and has come through time and time again for us. And as we do this – as we live in relationship with Jesus, trusting him for the outcome and handing the reins over to him – we will find that his amazing peace – peace so incredible we can't get our heads around it – will come and protect our minds and our hearts.

When I started doing my GCSEs I got so worked up about doing well that I suffered from panic attacks where I would hyperventilate and feel unwell. The morning before my third exam, I was reading the Bible and came across Psalm 57 which says 'My heart is steadfast, O God,' (v. 7). I felt challenged to trust in God rather than myself and repeated the psalm to myself during the exam as a way of reminding myself to look to Jesus rather than getting stressed. It helped me give my performance to God which gave me peace and I realised looking to ourselves only leads to heartache and stress.

Jessy

4

The Soft Heart
(Liza)

Blessed is the man who always fears the LORD,
but he who hardens his heart falls into trouble.

(Proverbs 28:14)

When we get hurt there's a seemingly natural reaction that occurs: we put up our defences to stop ourselves from getting hurt again. Sometimes, when it's a small pain, we don't even realise we do it; other times if we've been hurt more deeply, it's a very conscious decision as we vow we'll never let anything, or anyone, hurt us like that again.

Some of us have been dealt some heavy blows from life. The death of someone close to us. The breakdown of a relationship. The rejection of someone we thought loved us. Opening up to someone only to have them betray us. Pain inflicted by someone who was supposed to take care of us. The loss of a dream we thought was from God. It's hard to find anyone who's not been touched by pain. Life doesn't give us a choice about whether we suffer but we do get to choose how we deal with it. A fortress of protection may seem a sensible option but as the above proverb tells us, hardening our hearts only leads to trouble. God wants our hearts to stay soft and open to him.

Soft or weak?

I know I'm guilty of thinking if I have a soft heart it means I'm weak. I feel things really deeply and that means I'll cry at virtually anything. Good or bad, I'll shed a tear and it's a bit embarrassing when I'm left choking back a sob while watching an advert. You can imagine how I take things that are actually painful if I respond like that to a 60-second clip selling butter on TV. Honestly, I've sometimes despised the way I feel things so deeply because it leaves me feeling like a helpless mess. One of my major struggles in this area has been the fact I've been single for a really long time. A really long time. Many times I've got to the point where I've wanted to shut down my heart. I've begged God to be merciful and allow me to kill my desire, to shut it away deep down, so I can forget about it and stop having to face the pain of wanting something I don't have. Maybe there's been a similar situation in your life, a relationship – or lack of one – that makes you long to harden your heart. I don't know about you, but I do know every time I've been tempted to put a lid on things, God has challenged me to stay vulnerable. That means staying aware of my desire and my pain, and choosing to deal with it, rather than shutting down and growing cold.

God doesn't want us to harden our hearts. Not because he's cruel and enjoys watching us suffer but because that's not the way he designed us to be. He knows trying to ignore pain never makes it any better. We can push things so deep down we think they'll never see the light of day again, only to find they carry on affecting us and usually bubble up and explode in a messy way eventually. However well we think we've buried it, it just surfaces somewhere else in our lives, and usually leaves a trail of destruction. If I'd chosen to shut down my heart to ever being in a relationship then who knows where it would have led? It could be that I'd have become cynical about marriage and started to think of anyone who wanted a partner as needy. It could have been that every time a friend fell in love and got married, I became bitter rather than being able to rejoice with them. It could have been that I became more and more independent – turning away from my friends and trying to prove to myself (and everyone else) that I was fine on my own. It could have meant that when I eventually met someone, I wasn't open to the idea of marriage any more and so would have missed out on something good. Ultimately, the worst outcome would be that I would have shut down a piece of my heart to God.

When my boyfriend of four years and I broke up, I found it really hard. Things had been difficult for a while and he hurt me badly, so even though it was a mutual decision to end things, I was still in a lot of pain. I felt bitter towards him about the way he'd treated me, and angry about what had happened between us. I started to realise my heart was getting hard – like it was coated in bitterness – and it began to affect my relationship with God. I knew part of me was shutting down to God and I didn't want that. So I prayed God would help me forgive my ex and let go of the resentment. I felt an immediate shift in my heart, like I was back in the place where

God wanted me again just by submitting to him. After that, it was still sometimes a day-by-day choice to forgive and let go of the negative things, and remain open to God, but I knew my heart was a lot softer than it was.

Deborah

Disconnected from God

Even if we don't intentionally close ourselves off to God, the truth is we can't love and follow him fully if we're holding back a piece of our heart. As Ali was saying at the start of this book – our heart is absolutely central to how we see and respond to God. We're called to love God with all our heart, not just the bits with which we feel comfortable being vulnerable. Not that God doesn't understand that when things are painful we feel like it's our only form of protection – but he knows better. He knows we are safer when that pain is brought to him, not sealed behind a wall of glass. God wants us to be healed of all the things that hurt us and for that to happen we need to come before him and honestly express how we're feeling.

Hardening our hearts means we can become unresponsive to God, and the Bible links people hardening their hearts to them losing their ability to understand God and discern his ways. Ephesians 4:18 says, 'They are darkened in their understanding and separated

Hardening our hearts means we can become unresponsive to God.

from the life of God because of the ignorance that is in them due to the hardening of their hearts.'

And in chapter 8 of Mark's gospel we read how Jesus asked his disciples, 'Do you still not see or understand? Are your hearts hardened?' (See verse 17.) If we shut down our hearts we risk shutting down our ability to know and understand God.

The truth for some of us, however, is we have chosen to harden our hearts towards God because we believe *he* has let us down. When the Israelites had been in the desert a long time Psalm 95 tells us they hardened their hearts to God and rebelled against him because they didn't understand what was going on. They stopped trusting him and turned to their own ways. God may not lead us through a literal desert but most of us have known those times of pain and confusion, where we're not sure where God is, and what he's up to. We even wonder if he's forgotten us or left us behind in a dry and painful place. The Bible assures us God will never leave us or forsake us (Deuteronomy 31:6 and Hebrews 13:5) and we only have to look to the cross to know how deeply God loves us. The Bible is also quite clear we will have pain in this life (for example, Jesus said in John 16:33 we would have trouble in this world). No one ever promised it would be easy. In spite of this, we have a God who can keep our soft hearts safe. He can make us strong in the right way. Not defensive and bitter, people who carry around anger and resentment, but people of courage, people who are not beaten by circumstance, people who know they are in the care of a loving and merciful God.

For me, it has been a real challenge to keep my heart soft towards my dreams and longings. There are things I know God has called me to do but it's so tough when you're pushing doors, working hard and things aren't happening. God's continued to ask me to say 'yes' to him in this area and to wait for things to happen. It feels like it would almost be easier to just completely change direction, and forget how much of my life I've invested in these things, rather than keep pursuing something that's not happening. But God keeps whispering to me (often at the oddest times and places), reassuring me I'm on the right path, I'm doing the right thing, and that he is strategically placing me for all he has in store.

Jo

Compassion

Another reason God wants our hearts to stay soft is that a hard heart isn't compassionate. When we shut down our own pain we can end up not being moved by the pain of others, which will often keep us from acting to help them. The God we serve is a loving and compassionate God. Often, we look around us and we don't understand how God could love the world while it is in such a mess. But do we actually think God doesn't feel? That he sits in heaven watching us all quite dispassionately? The Bible shows us God feels things deeply: love, anger, jealousy, compassion. He's not immune to those things, he's moved and he wants us to be too. A number of times in the Bible we see God challenge his people because they aren't as tender-hearted as they should be.

Through the prophet Zechariah, God calls on his people to bring justice, show mercy, live compassionately and stop oppressing the poor. As these verses show, their hearts were hard:

> 'But they refused to pay attention; stubbornly they turned their backs and stopped up their ears. They made their hearts as hard as flint and would not listen to the law or to the words that the LORD Almighty had sent by his Spirit through the earlier prophets. So the LORD Almighty was very angry.' (Zechariah 7:11–12)

From the outside, it may have looked like the people were still following God as, just a few verses earlier, Zechariah talks of them fasting, mourning and celebrating God's feasts. Still, God knew their hearts and he saw they weren't truly doing it for him (see verse 5). They may have known God's commandments but their hearts weren't in it. Their hard hearts meant that as God was speaking to them they wouldn't listen and it made God furious.

In the New Testament, we see how much Jesus was a man characterised by compassion. Take a look at this passage:

> Jesus went into the synagogue again and noticed a man with a deformed hand. Since it was the Sabbath, Jesus' enemies watched him closely. If he healed the man's hand, they planned to accuse him of working on the Sabbath.
>
> Jesus said to the man with the deformed hand, 'Come and stand in front of everyone.' Then he turned to his critics and asked, 'Does the law permit good deeds on the Sabbath, or is it a day for doing evil? Is this a day to save life or to destroy it?' But they wouldn't answer him.

He looked around at them angrily and was deeply saddened by their hard hearts. Then he said to the man, 'Hold out your hand.' So the man held out his hand, and it was restored! (Mark 3:1–5, NLT)

Jesus is so clearly frustrated that, in the name of God, people would rather a man stay living with a deformed hand than see him healed on God's day. To try and live up to their standards of what they think God wants, they are acting against his character! It can seem ridiculous to us but then I'm sure we have many modern-day parallels. How often are we rushing around to do things for God and overlook someone who's in need of a chat? Do we look down on people when they confess their sins to us and make them feel unloved? We have our own standards, and can sometimes hold other values higher than compassion, but we need to stay soft so we are moved by that which moves God's heart.

> How often are we rushing around to do things for God and overlook someone who's in need of a chat?

I work with some quite broken people, and there are times I have realised I have given up hoping life will look different or brighter for them; maybe because they seem to keep being dealt some very difficult blows, or maybe because they keep making the same bad choices. Time and time again I have felt that urge from God to hope in him, in his love for them, and his future plans for them. My ongoing prayer is God will make me like an armadillo – thick-skinned and soft-hearted.

Sarah

Weakness

God wants our hearts to be compassionate and soft like his. It doesn't mean we're weak, like I've sometimes feared. It takes great strength of heart to love and, even though we get hurt, to keep loving. It takes great strength of character to face the tough realities of life on earth and remain soft to God's ways. We need strength to bring our pain before God, rather than trying to bury it; we need courage to live honestly with desire, rather than pretending it doesn't exist.

For many of us, hardening our hearts has been the only way we've known how to cope with life and we need to ask God to give us better ways of coping. We must be honest with God about the places in our hearts where we feel we've become hard. As we bring them to him, we submit to his will again, and give him permission to soften and restore our hearts. We need to soak in his presence and allow him to mould us to be more like him. When we are faced with situations that make us want to shut down, we need to choose to love and trust in our amazing and faithful God. If we stay soft, we stay open and able to receive all God has for us – his love, his grace, his mercy, his forgiveness and his kindness.

- A soft heart chooses to believe God loves, even when circumstances are hard.
- A soft heart stays turned towards God.
- A soft heart doesn't deny pain but deals with it openly before God.
- A soft heart carries no bitterness or anger but lets God bring healing.
- A soft heart is compassionate to others in need.
- A soft heart is capable of receiving love from others.

For the last two years of Junior School, some of my friends bullied me for being a Christian. I had been friends with them for years and, all of a sudden, they started taking the mick out of me for going to church and being different to them. Because they were my friends it felt like the people closest to me had rejected me for who I really was. After that, when I met new people I would hide my 'true' self and try to be the person I thought they wanted me to be. For each different group of people I knew, I would be a different person, but they soon saw through it and I found it was pretty tricky to keep it up too.

I felt if I let people get close to me, they would reject me once again. So I hardened my heart and pushed everyone away, including my true friends and my family. I found it very hard to love people because I thought they would hurt me. I hated to talk about my feelings or emotions because I was scared of being real with people. This even affected my relationship with God as I couldn't understand why he would love the real me when it felt like no one else did.

Over a few years, and after help from some amazing people, my heart began to soften and change. I realised the way I had been affected and was able to face these issues. It didn't happen overnight but, through a lot of prayer and support, I can now see that being myself is OK and that not everyone will reject me if I let them get close to me. My whole opinion about myself has changed and I know that I am accepted and loved by God for who I am. And that is the most important thing to me!

Martha

My mum suffers from an intense and long-term medical condition and, when I was thirteen, she was in so much pain one day it triggered severe depression in her. She made a semi-serious 'joke' that the only solution was for us as a family to make a suicide pact. I remember she had thought it through enough to have a plan for who would look after our dog without us. I started crying, and distinctly remember the fact that it made the situation much worse, and upset Mum more. I made a conscious decision never to cry again, as I didn't want to make things worse, or risk I wouldn't be trusted to cope with information about my mum's condition. I soon realised it was very hard not to cry! So I decided I was allowed to cry once a year, but only in secret like in the shower or under my duvet when everyone was asleep. I'm sure I still cried more than once a year but the situation had triggered in me the feeling that it was dangerous to show my emotions. For years, I would say, 'My heart is hidden under my ribs' as though that was a profound statement but really it just highlighted how desperate I was to keep my emotions private. When I was seventeen I went to the funeral of a girl who was just a couple of years older than me and I didn't cry at all. I felt guilty and began to realise how unhealthy suppressing my emotions was. I discovered I'd numbed my heart to feeling anything at all, and that meant I'd shut out good emotions like joy along with the pain. Over the years, God has challenged me about that and I've had to let go of the promise I made when I was thirteen. It helped me to pray through what happened with my mum and I've allowed God to soften me again so I can cry, laugh and express whatever emotions I am feeling.

Christina

Kat's story

I grew up in a Christian home with an incredible family who loved me and loved God. My parents took me to church, and I always knew what Christianity was, but I didn't understand it fully; I had the head knowledge but it wasn't alive in my heart. When I was thirteen my best friend, Hayley, was diagnosed with terminal cancer. She was given three months to live but died after just two. It all happened so quickly and I didn't understand any of it. I didn't know what cancer was, I didn't understand how someone so young could die, or how something so awful could happen to someone in my life. I didn't understand I couldn't just pick up the phone and talk to Hayley or invite her round for a sleepover. The moment my mum told me she had died, I went to my room, got under the covers and stayed there for hours. I felt so alone; where was God?

The funeral was beautiful. Hayley had a bright pink coffin, a bubble machine and, instead of hymns, we sang 'Lion King' songs. But then, after the service, came the part where we went to the crematorium; it was the first time I ever experienced what felt like true darkness. I felt lost and helpless. My heart was being torn apart and, as I stood looking at her coffin, I made a vow. I promised myself I would never feel that way again. I never wanted to let myself hurt as deeply as I was in that moment, I didn't want to ever feel so low or experience so much pain. It was an incredibly stupid promise to make at thirteen but at the time it felt logical. I just couldn't handle that level of pain and I didn't realise making that promise meant I would have to shut out the world. I figured the best way to avoid getting hurt was to not let anyone close enough to hurt me. So I let my heart go hard, and I didn't realise toughening up my heart on the inside would impact my outward behaviour so dramatically.

I lived with a hard heart for years and I pushed my family and my friends away to try to protect myself. Just after I turned fourteen my brother, and then my mum, both had to have operations and were in wheelchairs, and I began to feel like everything in my life was out of my control. I started missing school, drinking heavily and taking drugs. But still I wanted more control so I turned to sex. It felt like it gave me back the authority over my own life which had been taken away when Hayley died. It meant I had control over men; I could control what I did with my body in a way I couldn't control what else happened. Sleeping around gave me a reputation as a 'bad girl who didn't let anything bother her' and I felt like I was succeeding at keeping people away and reducing my chances of getting hurt again. I didn't have a boyfriend at the time, because I didn't want to get close to anyone and I found more power in having lots of different guys chasing after me. For a time, it felt like I was back in control: I was independent and doing what I wanted, when I wanted. Then the sex started to feel pointless and no longer made me feel powerful, but I realised I couldn't stop. I had become addicted to sex. I felt worthless and alone, the things I thought would satisfy my heart had made me miserable, and I was totally broken. I became extremely low, and for a long time I seriously struggled with self-harm and bulimia. Bulimia was another way I tried to control something in my life and I started to self-harm because, for a short time after I cut myself, I could focus on the pain of the cut and block out any other painful feelings. I was hurting in so many ways: my life was chaos, all because my heart was so hurt.

After years of living like this, I went to a Soul Survivor festival, and was dragged by my friends to a 'Soul Sista' seminar on identity. While I was there I finally realised I couldn't carry on living in such a destructive way. It was the way the speaker talked about the joy of living a life being loved by God that made me understand I was living the opposite. I was suddenly desperate for God and to know his love. I was desperate for his healing touch and he gave it. I got on my knees and, while someone prayed for me, I cried for ages, all the tears I should have cried when Hayley died but hadn't let myself cry. In that moment, I met a God who heals and loves. I let God put my heart back together and left the seminar a changed person. God completely broke into the addictions that had a hold on me, and healed me from the grief and pain I had been holding onto.

Life carried on, but this time I knew I wasn't alone. We began to rebuild our family life and I felt God call me to change schools where I met some incredible people. Then I got into a relationship, which lasted around two years and turned out to be pretty awful. My boyfriend physically and sexually abused me, manipulated me, and would constantly mess with my emotions. I just couldn't understand why this was happening to me. I had been doing so well, my life had finally come together, and then this? I ended up more broken than I had ever been. For a long time, once the relationship ended, and I found the strength to walk away, I was depressed. I would get up, eat breakfast, then go back to sleep because I was hurting too much to be awake. I eventually tried to overdose. I just wanted the memories of the relationship to go, but as I sat in hospital with my parents, God met with me again. He showed me his loving arms. He showed me he could restore me wholly and fully, that he could make me pure again, and that no matter what, he had always been holding my heart in his hands. After this, I started to bring all of my pain to God every day, and, slowly but surely, he healed me and continues to heal me today. God came to my rescue and filled me with his love.

But it was still a process. I had so much stuff I needed to deal with. The guy I had been with used to frequently call me horrible names, and I had heard them so much I had started to believe they were true. I had to actively choose to believe God's truth about who I am instead, so I would wake up every morning, look in the mirror and say 'God loves me, just as I am.'

Looking back at it all now, I can see the repercussions of my decision to harden my heart. I thought I was protecting myself from pain but, in actual fact, I found myself in so much more pain. I realise now, when we harden our hearts, we not only shut out people, but we shut out God. God wants our hearts soft because he longs for an intimate relationship with us and he wants us to know how loved we are. In letting God soften my heart, I have found true joy and freedom which I never thought was possible, and I have found a love that has completely transformed my heart.

5

The Satisfied Heart
(Ali)

> 'The heart is hopelessly dark and deceitful,
> a puzzle that no one can figure out.
> But I, God, search the heart
> and examine the mind.
> I get to the heart of the human.
> I get to the root of things.
> I treat them as they really are,
> not as they pretend to be.'
>
> (Jeremiah 17:9–10, *The Message*)

All humans are made to live in communion with God, and yet here we are, living in a fallen world. We don't know the perfect joy that comes from him every day; we don't feel surrounded by his unending love; we don't live in the complete peace of Jesus. Yes, we see glimpses of these things, but they just remind us we were made for more than this world and they make our hearts yearn for that fulfilment. In short, our hearts are hungry for more.

However, as Jeremiah points out in the verses above, our hearts are 'hopelessly deceitful' so on a day-to-day basis we probably don't spend time thinking about how desperate we are for God's presence. If we've been to church recently, read our Bibles and prayed a bit, that's often enough to make us feel like that box is ticked. We're still hungry but we're not aware of where our true hunger lies. Instead, our hearts confuse us by making us hunger and thirst for other things. They tell us we want one thing when actually we want another.

The same has been true of humans since we were created. In the book of Exodus we read time and time again how God's people looked to other idols to meet their needs. Take the Israelites' story in Exodus where Moses is in the habit of going up the mountain to meet with God and then coming back and relaying what he's said to everyone. It seems to be quite a good system for a while, but in chapter 32, we read Moses was once taking a while to return, and the people started getting twitchy. They wondered if he was ever coming and so they asked Aaron to make a god for them. They were so desperate they made a golden calf out of their earrings to worship – it's crazy! Reading the story it's easy to think, 'But God has just freed you from slavery, parted the Red Sea for you, led you by pillars of cloud and fire; and fed you with manna from heaven. How could you doubt him? How could you be so desperate that you turned to a golden calf for fulfilment instead of God?' Though they had seen God do great things they were like starving children who couldn't resist snacking before their real meal came along; they needed something to fill the void. But, before I get too smug and annoyed with them, I have to remember how often I do the same thing. I don't have a golden calf tucked away to worship when I'm feeling in need, but I do let other things sneak into my life, and try to placate my hunger for God. Whether it's keeping busy, choosing something nice to eat, doing a quick shopping trip or diving head first into a DVD box set, there are plenty of golden calf replacements around.

There are so many things we use to fill the hunger in our hearts. Sometimes, they bring feelings of joy, exhilaration and satisfaction. That may last or it may fade when we realise it didn't really answer the cry of our heart. Sometimes, we satisfy our hunger with destructive things and we find ourselves feeling ashamed, guilty, disappointed or empty. Turning to God in our hunger brings true freedom – but to do that we first have to recognise the signs that our heart is hungry.

Signs of a hungry heart

Not long after I was first married, I found myself one evening feeling out of sorts. I felt quite emotional and needy so I went to my husband Joel, hoping he'd look after me and make me feel better. We'd been together long enough that he was wise to my ways and he simply said, 'Ali, I don't have what you need, Jesus does. Go to him.' I'll be honest; it felt like a slap in the face and I wanted to punch him right back! How dare he not look after me when I was feeling vulnerable? Wasn't that his role as my husband? Furious, I went to Jesus in a bit of a strop, but then stopped, and tried to wait in his presence. I poured out my heart and told God how I had been feeling that day, and started to unravel some of what was going on in my heart and my head making me feel upset. Amazingly, afterwards, I didn't feel quite so needy; there was a peace in my heart that hadn't been there before. If Joel had tried to make me feel better, he'd have helped me cover up some of the discomfort in my heart, but it wouldn't have helped me get to the bottom of what was going on, or provided more than a bandage over the problem. Annoyingly, instead of being able to hit Joel, I had to go back to him and say thank you that he hadn't tried to fill the gap that was God's to fill.

Relationships were never designed to take the place of our relationship with God.

That said, relationships are a gift from God. They can be a massive blessing and God often shows us his love and care through our families, friends, boy-friends or husbands. What we need to remember is they were never designed to take the place of our relationship with God. We can easily look to those relationships to be the answer to our problems, and be quick to go to those people God has given us, rather than God himself. We should never neglect the main source, or expect anyone else to satisfy us. Not only does it put too much pressure on that relationship, it's just not possible for one human to meet all of our needs.

There are plenty of other ways we try and fill the gaps in our hearts, and these will be different things for all of us. What provides comfort for some will do nothing for others, so we all need to look at our own behaviour to recognise the outward signs of our internal hunger.

See if you can relate to any of these. Do you:

- Shop, shop, shop even when you don't need anything just to get a buzz?
- Desperately want to attract the attention of the opposite sex?
- Find yourself feeling insecure, anxious or panicky for no obvious reason?

- Eat too much or not enough?
- Push yourself to work too hard when it comes to exercise?
- Get involved in unhealthy relationships or sexual activity?
- Regularly drink too much alcohol?
- Have an addiction you can't seem to break free from?
- Feel desperate for attention, compliments and/or recognition?

As Jeremiah said, the heart is deceitful. We find ourselves in a time of pain and our thoughts turn to a new coat, a slab of cake or a couple of drinks to make ourselves feel better. Occasionally, those things are OK; this is not about denying ourselves any earthly pleasure. But some of those things can become addictive and destructive. They can become idols that don't satisfy but enslave us, stop us from going to God and leave us feeling worse than we did originally. What I'm trying to encourage us to do is to look at things we consistently turn to that might have more of a hold on us than they should. One of the ways to work out if something is controlling us is to examine why we want the thing we do, and to look at what happens if we don't get it.

Exploring the heart

Fasting – from food or from something else we rely on – is one of the key disciplines in the Christian faith that helps us discover what's really going on in our hearts and helps us to master our desires. When you identify an unhealthy habit you're feeding, think about fasting from it. Don't set yourself a potentially impossible challenge of giving it up cold turkey and never touching it again; think about going without it for a bit to see what happens – even if it's just delaying by holding off satisfying that desire for half an hour. What happens if you wait? This can be one of the best exercises to reveal what's going on in our hearts. When desire is awakened, just stop and examine your feelings. What rises up? If you are using something to mask a bigger issue that thing will start raising its head pretty soon. Sometimes, you have to starve your heart to get to the bottom of what's going on. You have to let yourself feel the hunger and explore it, rather than feeding it immediately.

Of course, we don't have to do this exploration alone! Jeremiah reminds us God examines our hearts and minds, and he sees what's actually happening. If we let him, he'll take us on a journey to understand what's taking place too. Sometimes, going to God will change everything and we'll feel so much better afterwards. Sometimes, there will be a quick answer and revelation as to what is going on in our hearts and God will give us some immediate action we need to think about. Other times, it will take bringing the issues consistently before God, and talking and praying with wise friends, to get to the root of things. Because, sadly, even bringing something to God isn't a magic wand! If you've been through a painful situation and had someone blithely say 'offer it to God' you'll know it's not always that simple. Occasionally, God changes our hearts in one miraculous moment. More often than that, it's a process of simply dealing with hard stuff in God's presence, rather than having him remove the hunger or pain entirely.

One thing we know for sure is whatever we're going through that's making us hungry, God wants to be in it with us. (After all, he is Emmanuel: God with us.) He gave up everything to relate to us, to show us he understood our pain. We sometimes feel like we need to sort things out on our own, instead, let's let him be God with us in our pain. Even in our moments of agony, when it can seem tempting to push him away (especially if we want to use our back-up plan to cover our hurt), what we need is to be honest with God and say, 'Life is really tough at the moment but I invite you into that.' It's better we're facing up to what's making us miserable in God's loving embrace, than looking for answers in the wrong places.

I went through a stage where I couldn't bear the thought of not having food if I wanted it. Not just at mealtimes, but throughout the day. If I even glanced at something and the thought entered my head that I might like it, it would be in my mouth before my thought process had gone much further. I knew it wasn't good for me and asked God what was going on. He showed me that in lots of other areas of my life I couldn't have the things I wanted. I felt like many of my basic needs were going unmet each day, so when I found a 'need', or rather a desire, I could meet (in the form of food) I wasn't able to say no. Knowing that stopped me from feeling powerless in the face of my desire. It didn't mean I always had the ability to say no but it helped me bring things before God and deal with the bigger issues of unmet needs.

Helen

Our daily bread

I find it interesting Jesus told us to pray for our daily bread. Like God's people in the desert when he gave them manna – he didn't want to give them enough so they would be OK for a month and then check in with him then. He wants us on a short leash to keep us by his side because that's where we are safest. Our daily bread is so many things – yes, it's the food we eat, but for many of us living in the Western world, we're fairly sure we've got enough money for the next meal. We may however be desperate for God's love when we feel lonely. We may need God's peace when our hearts are frantic with worry. Maybe you need that daily reminder God knows and loves you. Maybe you need to be reassured of your worth if you feel insecure. Whatever it is, we need to be asking God to feed our hearts daily and to give us what we need for that day, then coming back to him tomorrow and asking for the same.

This side of heaven there will always be a hunger in our hearts because we're not living with God in the way we were made to. We're going to experience things like loneliness, fear and insecurity sometimes, and all we can do is stay as close to him as possible. The reality is we will probably fail to do that and we will turn to these other 'idols' to comfort us from time to time. I don't say that to be pessimistic or to endorse that we don't try, but simply so we don't get caught in a cycle of guilt that makes us feel trapped. The temptation is to think, 'Right, I'm going to conquer this.' We stir ourselves up, convince ourselves things will change, then we inevitably fall sooner or later, and wind up feeling defeated and out of control. The idea of daily bread acknowledges the hunger comes back; we don't eat once and find ourselves forever satisfied, it's a continual process. Part of the maturing of our faith isn't learning to stand on our own two feet, it's learning to be utterly dependent on God to meet our needs.

Practical things we can do

There are some practical ways we can help ourselves when dealing with these issues.

Don't feed your appetite

The more we know ourselves, the better we become at recognising what will feed our hunger too. It's so obvious in one sense, but in another we're so used to having some of these things around us, or as part of our lives, we stop realising the effect they are having on us. For example:

- Romantic films or books can fuel a craving for intimacy, love and romance.
- Spending time in shopping centres or reading fashion magazines can lead to a desire for more clothes and belongings.
- Sexually explicit movies feed lust.
- Comparing ourselves to others (whether in terms of gifts, opportunities or general lifestyle) will often leave us feeling like we're lacking in some way.

If we struggle with shopping there's no point in standing in the middle of a huge shopping centre asking God to take away our hunger. We're just making it harder for ourselves when we put ourselves in the path of temptation. Don't work up an appetite. Know the things that make you hungry and where possible avoid them. If there are situations you can't avoid, then ask someone to pray with you before you go into them, and hold yourself accountable to them about your behaviour. Knowing in advance you will have to tell someone what you did really helps dull your desire to do something you shouldn't!

I used to love reading fashion magazines; I've always had a passion for clothes and I loved looking through all the gorgeous stuff every month. Then I found that the magazines stirred in me a desire for more things – I would close the magazine and be distinctly aware of all the things I wanted and lacked in my life, rather than thankful for all the amazing things I did have. I stopped reading the magazines and soon found that my desire for new things went down accordingly.

Anne

Accountability

Sometimes, we're oblivious to our sin and weaknesses and it takes others to point it out, like King David. After he had slept with Bathsheba, had her husband killed and then married her, David is visited by the prophet Nathan. Nathan starts telling David a story about a rich man, a poor man and some sheep, but we all know what he's actually talking about: he's calling David on his sin. David, on the other hand, is completely oblivious. He's outraged by the story and demands justice is done, not realising he is condemning himself. You see, in order for David to have not only slept with Bathsheba, but gone on to kill Uriah and take her as his own, he had to be in some way detached from his heart.

The things we use to fill our hungry hearts may not be as extreme as David's but they can still cause us to detach, even slightly, in order to keep doing them. I used to use shopping as a coping mechanism. I didn't feel good about myself and the way I looked, but I found when I was wearing new clothes, I'd feel better and people would

God never meant for
us to do this life alone.

give me more compliments. I used to shop frequently and spend more money than I had, but I convinced myself what I was doing was fine. I didn't want to confront what was really going on so I tried not to think about my actions. This went on for a while until a couple of close friends challenged me and stopped me in my tracks. They asked me what was happening in my heart that made me feel the need to shop, and it was the first time I couldn't avoid thinking about it. There wasn't a quick fix in that conversation, but I'm so glad they didn't let my behaviour carry on un-checked, as it started the process for me to deal with my issues.

This is just one of many reasons why it's healthy for us to be in relationships where people know what is actually going on with us. Accountability can be a bit of a buzz word, but what it really means is developing relationships where nothing is hidden. God never meant for us to do this life alone – so pick safe and trustworthy friends who will love, support and challenge you to help you grow. It's a good idea to give someone permission to challenge you if they see unhealthy behaviours in your life; most of us aren't brave enough to come right out and say it unless someone has asked. Left hidden these things can rot away at us from inside. They can lead to addictions, pain, breakdown of relationships, drive wedges in our relationship with God and others, and can tie us into a feeling of failure. Talking to others and talking to God brings things out into the light where the devil can't use it against us. Have you ever felt trapped by your actions? Afraid that if someone knew the truth they would see you differently or worried that God can't use you because of some pattern of behaviour in your life? Speaking to someone is often a massive step in breaking the power of that thing.

God doesn't want us to be controlled by anything. He has given us so many amazing gifts and blessings in our lives, but when we try and set them up as idols they will fail us, and try to control us instead. His design is for us to live in freedom where we can enjoy the gifts he has given without being trapped by them. As we learn to recognise the places where our hearts are hungry and in need, we will learn how to come to him for what we need, as there we'll find our hearts satisfied.

6

The Hopeful Heart
(Liza)

May the God of hope fill you with all joy and peace as you trust in him, so that you may overflow with hope by the power of the Holy Spirit.

(Romans 15:13)

Even if you're not a hugely enthusiastic football fan you'll know what I mean when I say that in the run-up to a World Cup or European championship the country starts buzzing. There's a sense of excitement and hope. Everywhere you go there are St George's Cross flags, and pictures of the latest football stars wearing their shirts with pride, looks of determination on their faces. There's a fever, a great anticipation of what it would be like to watch our captain lift that trophy, knowing how happy it would make so many people. Conversation is full of plans of where to watch matches and talk of historic victories. People hold off celebrating events like birthdays and even weddings so they don't clash with those all important matches. Anticipation builds and we wait, hoping this will be our year.

Inevitably, a short while later, there's quite a different picture. Incomplete wall charts hang off the wall, parks are again busy with people remembering there's more to a summer than sitting inside watching sport. And there's an air of gloom. Why did we think it would be any different this time? Why haven't we learnt from our past? Why do we have such an appalling penalties record? We had hope. Our dreams came tumbling down as the England boys got on that plane back home. We are crushed. But will we do it again? Of course we will! Two years later when the next championship starts, that same fever starts sweeping the nation. Sport is no fun without hope. Neither is life.

In our cynical world, we sometimes lose heart and think it's better not to hope at all than to hope, and then face disappointment. George Bernard Shaw said in his play *Caesar and Cleopatra*, 'He who has never hoped can never despair.'[1] And we'd all like to avoid despair, wouldn't we? No one likes to dream only to see those dreams crushed. So, sometimes, we're tempted to buy into the wisdom that if we just numb our hearts, set our sights incredibly low, we won't ever have to be disappointed. Often, it happens when something hasn't turned out quite the way we wanted, something we were passionate about, something that meant a lot to us. A little voice starts saying, 'I don't ever want to feel this pain again. Next time, I won't expect as much and I won't be left feeling this upset.' I know I've been there – haven't you? However, one of the things God seems particularly keen on is that we are hopeful and he himself is referred to as 'the God of hope' (Romans 15:13). In the same breath, Paul prays we would 'overflow with hope

---

[1] G. Bernard Shaw, *Three Plays for Puritans* (London: Penguin, 2006), Act IV. Used by permission of The Society of Authors on behalf of the Bernard Shaw Estate.

by the power of the Holy Spirit'. So why is hope so important? Martin Luther King summed it up brilliantly when he said, 'If you lose hope, somehow you lose the vitality that keeps life moving, you lose that courage to be, that quality that helps you go on in spite of it all.'[2]

Anyone who's felt hopeless will testify to the truth in that statement. When hope is lost we feel like we're dying. We can go through the motions of being alive but we have no enthusiasm, no passion and no purpose. Surely that's not how God created us to be? It's like we can't truly live without hope. I don't believe for one second he created us to live these guarded lives, going about with numb hearts that fear hope in case of disappointment.

Deferred hope

Often, when we talk about hope, we give stories and examples about how people waited, hoped and eventually got what it was they were hoping for. These stories are helpful and encouraging, and remind us God so often gives us the things we're longing for – whether that's a relationship, a job, a qualification, healing or whatever it may be for us. These stories build our faith and we need to hear them.

But what about when we're struggling? When we haven't had our happy ending yet? In Proverbs 13:12 we're told 'Hope deferred makes the heart sick'. Anyone who's ever waited and waited, hoped and hoped, and not yet seen things resolved will know the truth of that statement. When we long for things and they don't materialise we lose heart, we get weary and we can feel like all the life is draining right out of us. Where do we go then? The only

---

[2] http://thinkexist.com/quotation

thing we can do is go back to God with our hopes, dreams and fears. Bring them to his loving arms and ask for him to restore us again.

As I mentioned when we were looking at trust, over seven years ago I left my job in Public Relations with this crazy idea that God was asking me to write. In particular, I felt like I should write a novel. It took me a while to believe that was actually what God wanted but eventually I got on and finished it. I was full of hope; I knew God had spoken to me, I knew I had done my bit and taken a significant step of faith, so surely all I had to do was sit back and wait for the miracle to happen? Apparently not. Getting a novel published is almost impossible. Publishers don't have time to work with new writers so you have to go through an agent. A good agent gets about 300 unsolicited manuscripts every week and takes on about one or two new writers a year. I'm not a betting person but I'd say those odds were pretty bad. So, one by one, the rejections came back. Sometimes, they'd have positive comments and a little flame of hope would flicker, other times it seemed like my work hadn't even been read, and a huge bucket of water would douse that tiny flame. Eventually, I decided to write a second novel and am currently looking to get that published but I couldn't have done that without hope. By myself, I would have just given up, told myself it was a ridiculous dream and tried to forget about it, but God wanted me to remain hopeful about what he'd asked me to do, so I went ahead and wrote the second book. I've had so many times when my heart has felt sick, when I've received another rejection and thought 'Why am I putting myself through this? Will this ever amount to anything other than pain?'

Ultimately, this has made me question, what am I really hoping in? Where am I putting my hope? I felt like

We don't put our hope in the things we want, we hope in God himself.

God told me to write a book but I didn't hear him say it would be published. So my hope shouldn't be in the outcome of my actions, but in my faithful loving Father.

For me, this is the key question when it comes to the subject of hope. God is not asking us to 'think positively' or 'dream unrealistically', and just put up with it when things don't work out as we'd hoped (after all, no one's likely to get everything they wish for in life, and it would probably cause us nothing but problems if we did). The key thing is **we don't put our hope in the things we want, we hope in God himself**. We hope in who he is, in what he has promised us, and in his unending and unfailing love, mercy and grace. If we just hope for the things we want we will end up with sick hearts. If we hope in *him* – in the belief he can use any circumstance for his glory and our good (Romans 8:28) – there is always reason to hope.

This also means we need to be careful not to base our hope on our own abilities. If we're feeling fairly confident it's easy to start thinking we have things under control. You ace your exams and you're sure you'll get into the university you want; you work hard and are certain you'll be next in line for a pay rise or promotion. In the end, though, it is God who determines our steps and the outcomes in our lives:

No king is saved by the size of his army;
no warrior escapes by his great strength.

A horse is a vain hope for deliverance;
despite all its great strength it cannot save.
But the eyes of the LORD are on those who fear him,
on those whose hope is in his unfailing love,
to deliver them from death
and keep them alive in famine.

We wait in hope for the LORD;
he is our help and our shield.
In him our hearts rejoice,
for we trust in his holy name.
May your unfailing love rest upon us, O LORD,
even as we put our hope in you. (Psalm 33:16–22)

We're highly unlikely to be going into battle on a horse but there's still truth in this passage for us. Anything that we put our hope in above God is in vain; he is the one who delivers us, changes things and orders our lives.

Hope in God's promises

I have learnt over the last few years that God is our hope, whatever our situation and however hopeless, dark or bleak it may seem. There have been times where I have sat alongside friends who have been trapped in addiction for many years and are in the darkest of places, when suddenly God has given me hope for a different way of life for them. Being able to share that hope with someone in pain is like shining a light in darkness, and can bring amazing transformation. Some of these friends are what many people would call 'hopeless', but I know there's no such thing as 'hopeless' in God's kingdom. Hope isn't always the most natural response, when you look at the circumstances, but when I've lifted my eyes up to Jesus, and seen the bigger picture, I'm able to hope again. I think it is as we spend time with God, that we receive his hope and we are able to share it with others.

Emily

Sometimes God does give us specific promises and asks us to hope in them until we see them come to pass. Because of his nature we can be sure that if he makes us a promise, he will fulfil it. Look at how Paul talks about Abraham to the Romans:

> Against all hope, Abraham in hope believed and so became the father of many nations, just as it had been said to him, 'So shall your offspring be.' Without weakening in his faith, he faced the fact that his body was as good as dead – since he was about a hundred years old – and that Sarah's womb was also dead. Yet he did not waver through unbelief regarding the promise of God, but was strengthened in his faith and gave glory to God, being fully persuaded that God had power to do what he had promised. (Romans 4:18–21)

Paul was using Abraham as an example to say that sometimes what God promises us seems completely crazy and illogical, but God is able. We too can draw many examples from the Bible of people who believed God could do anything and saw him do amazing miracles. I love how Paul says, 'Against all hope, Abraham in hope believed'. It's like saying everything was looking utterly hopeless from an earthly point of view, and Abraham faced up to that fact, but he still chose hope and faith because he knew the God who had made the promise to him was capable. When I read that, it makes me want to be one of those people who is 'fully persuaded that God has power to do what he had promised'. If we are fully persuaded then we too will be people who hope in God's promises, people who believe he 'is able to do immeasurably more than all we ask or imagine' (Ephesians 3:20).

What if God hasn't spoken to us specifically like he did with Abraham? Well, as the psalmist says, 'In his word I put my hope' (Psalms 130:5). We have the whole Bible which speaks God's words to us, and we can hope and trust in those promises. Ultimately, putting our hope in God's promises is about putting our hope in his character. Our hope should be in him as that's the only safe place for it. I've misunderstood this so many times; I've thought God was asking

Ultimately, putting our hope in God's promises is about putting our hope in his character.

me to be hopeful about a situation only to find that my circumstances hadn't changed. For my writing, I need to be hopeful that someday there could be a breakthrough, otherwise I wouldn't be able to do it. But, ultimately, my hope has to be that God knows best and he has plans for me. He will use me, and the difficult circumstances in my life, to make me more like him. I have to trust that by leading me along this path he intends no harm for me and, even if I never see one of my novels published, God can and will give my life and my work purpose.

Unending hope

When I left college and needed a job, I found myself
driving past a big local company and suddenly just
'knew' I was going to work for them. I wrote to the
HR department asking if any jobs were available
and they wrote back saying they had nothing. The
weird thing was, God had given me such hope I
was going to work there, that I knew it would happen. I didn't even bother applying for anything else!
I drove my parents mad as I sat around for six
weeks until a letter arrived from the company asking me to come in for interview. I got the job and
worked there for the next two and a half years. In
that situation I didn't struggle to have hope at all,
because God spoke more clearly than I think I've
ever heard him, all I had to do was hope in his faith-
fulness, and hold on to receive what he'd already
promised.

Ali

Recently, I've heard some heartbreaking stories of
Christians facing terminal illness. People who care for
and love those people have spent much time reassuring
them with Bible verses that promise full and miraculous
healing. Whilst there is most definitely a time and a
place for this, and I certainly believe that God can and
does heal people, we have to know that even in death
there is great hope for us. As Christians we should not
only have hope in spite of death but *because* of death.
The trouble is, we seem to have lost sight of what awaits
us on the other side. Even as I write this, I am aware

what a painful topic death will be to so many of you reading this. Maybe you've recently lost someone you love or are watching them fight for their lives. Please hear me when I say I'm not pretending this is easy. We should fight for life, pray for healing and grieve for the loss of health and life. What I am saying is we should listen to Paul who said to the Corinthians:

> If only for this life we have hope in Christ, we are to be pitied more than all men. (1 Corinthians 15:19)

Or as The Message puts it:

> 'If all we get out of Christ is a little inspiration for a few short years, we're a pretty sorry lot'.

Paul is trying to get us to see past the things we know now, the things we can touch, smell and see here, and think about what awaits for us in heaven. He continues:

> The sun has one kind of splendour, the moon another and the stars another; and star differs from star in splendour. So will it be with the resurrection of the dead. The body that is sown is perishable, it is raised imperishable; it is sown in dishonour, it is raised in glory; it is sown in weakness, it is raised in power; it is sown a natural body, it is raised a spiritual body. (1 Corinthians 15:41–44)

We value the life we live, rightly so, as it is a gift from God, but we mustn't get fooled into believing this is as good as it gets. Because of what Jesus did for us on the cross, we get to spend eternity with our loving heavenly Father. That's something to celebrate! Everything will be different the other side of heaven and it will be better. Paul tells us we will be raised to a new life in power and glory: what we have here is just a shadow of what is to come.

> For to me, to live is Christ and to die is gain. If I am to go on living in the body, this will mean fruitful labour for me. Yet what shall I choose? I do not know! I am torn between the two: I desire to depart and be with Christ, which is better by far; but it is more necessary for you that I remain in the body. (Philippians 1:21–24)

Most of us have these slightly odd visions of heaven that don't inspire us to want to be there – eternity in a dull church service? No thank you! But Paul grasps the concept of heaven so well he says he'd rather die than live. He says being dead in the body so he is fully alive in Christ is 'better by far'. Not fifty-fifty or much the same, but better by a long shot.

It's a tragedy that when believers are facing terminal illnesses the only hope we feel we can offer them is the hope of God's healing. Because we shouldn't have to fear death. We don't have to hope only in our days on earth. Of course, that's not to say we don't pray for healing. We can and we should, and it's right to hope for healing. However, we must also know we can rest assured, even in the face of death, that God is victorious. Death holds no sting for the believer, as Paul says to the Corinthians:

> 'Death has been swallowed up in victory.'
> 'Where, O death, is your victory?
> Where, O death, is your sting?'
> The sting of death is sin, and the power of sin is the law. But thanks be to God! He gives us the victory through our Lord Jesus Christ. (1 Corinthians 15:54–57)

As Christians we have the ultimate hope: we have hope even in the face of death. But let's not forget we have so much hope for this life too. God works all things together for the good of those who love him (Romans 8:28) so whatever we're facing today, let's ask God to bring us his perspective. Let's ask him to fill us with hope again: hope in his amazing promises, hope in his word and hope in him – our loving, unchanging Father.

If we have a hopeful heart we will:

- Be like the woman in Proverbs 31 who can 'laugh at the days to come' (v. 25).
- Take action. When we hope we have reason to act.
- Hold our head up high.
- Embrace all God has created us to be.
- Be persistent in prayer.
- Be free from apathy and cynicism.
- Experience joy.

A few years ago I was involved in a car accident. Though the incident was pretty small, the damage was bad in that I suffered from chronic back and neck pain. Some days, I couldn't move and was in agony, I was limited in all the things I'd loved doing. Carrying a bag was a nightmare; swimming became a no go; even holding my newborn godson was sometimes impossible. One thing I really missed was dancing in church. I loved to worship God in that way. Doctors weren't always helpful and most people said 'Once you've hurt your back, that's it for life', which wasn't particularly encouraging. I prayed and prayed for healing – some days it felt better, then other days it felt worse.

Ultimately, as I spent time with God I realised there was always hope. Even if I wasn't free of the pain until I got to heaven, I knew I would one day be done with the pain and able to worship God freely.

Elizabeth

7

The Surrendered Heart
(Liza)

> But your hearts must be fully committed to the LORD our
> God, to live by his decrees and obey his commands.
>
> (1 Kings 8:61)

Hands up if you like being in control. Mine is waving in the
air right now. I like it when I can be in charge, and do want
I want when I want. But, when I became a Christian I said
that I was 'giving my life to God'. This isn't just a nice little
phrase without much meaning, it means I was promising
to relinquish control of my own life and give it over to God.
Eek. That's hugely significant and, it's probably fair to say,
I had no idea how huge at the time. Many of us call ourselves Christians but still want to have control over our
own lives. God addresses this in the book of Isaiah:

> The Lord says:
> 'These people come near to me with their mouth
> and honour me with their lips,
> but their hearts are far from me.
> Their worship of me
> is made up only of rules taught by men.' (29:13)

What he's saying here is that it's not enough to go through the motions of having a relationship with God. He's just not interested in us being half-hearted Christians who sing the songs on a Sunday but do whatever we like the rest of the week, making our own choices and living however we choose. We can all put on a good outward appearance – turn up at church and say the right things, but it literally counts for nothing if that's not what's in our hearts.

God wants our whole hearts, and this is exactly what Jesus said when he was asked what the greatest commandment is:

> 'Love the Lord your God with all your heart and with all your soul and with all your mind.' (Matthew 22:37–38)

The first thing for us to stop and think about here is the fact that this is about love. Yes, we're talking about obedience, but it should come out of a place of love, not fear or duty or anything else. We're told in 1 John 4:19 'We love because he first loved us', which is important. We don't have to summon up love out of nowhere, forcing ourselves like robots into believing we love God, we just have to respond to his love for us. We don't have to woo him to get his attention – he's there, always, waiting for us to listen and hear him say he loves us.

When we love God with our whole heart it means we don't put anyone or anything before him. Jesus warns we can't love God and money (Matthew 6:24) because our hearts are then divided between two masters. The same is true of just about anything. We can't love God as he deserves to be loved if we put another relationship before him, whether that's love of a parent, a sibling, a child, a spouse or a friend – anyone! Similarly, we can't love God with our whole hearts if our first priority is our 'calling', one of the gifts we have been given or a hobby we love. Nothing should come before him.

It's not that God doesn't want us to love these people and these things in our life: it's that he knows life works best when we prioritise him. When we love him and receive his love for us, he is the one who enables us to love other people effectively.

Love and obedience

In 2 John 1:6 we read that 'this is love: that we walk in obedience to his commands.'

Obeying God is one of the ways we show we love him; simply doing the things he asks us to do. This may be something big or something small, but each and every day we should be looking to follow his ways and not our own. If you don't know God very well, hearing him say he wants everything could sound quite controlling. As we catch glimpses of his character through his word, and during our relationship with him, we know he's not trying to oppress us. He knows the path to true freedom is for us to follow his ways, his choices – he knows that is the best thing for us and he wants the best for us because he loves us.

Obeying God is one of the ways we show we love him.

There are some amazing examples in the Bible of people who were obedient to God at great cost to themselves, but at great gain for God's kingdom. For instance, when an angel shows up out of nowhere and tells Mary she's going to have a baby, even though she's a virgin, she doesn't argue or complain. Instead, she submits to his plans, saying, 'I am the Lord's servant . . . May it be to me as you have said' (Luke 1:38). The Bible doesn't tell us a great deal about how Mary felt but I imagine she was somewhat scared! Not least of all at the thought of having to tell her husband-to-be, her family and everyone who knew her that she hadn't been misbehaving while she was engaged, but was giving birth to the Messiah by way of the Holy Spirit. Try living that one down. Mary's obedience is humbling – the task asked of her was huge; it changed the whole of her future, risking her reputation, her relationships and her heart, but she said yes. The passage tells us God chose her because she had found great favour with him (v. 28) and, probably, it's fair to say because God knew her heart, he knew she would say yes to him. As God looks at the earth today, searching for people who will do his will, would he be able to ask you, knowing that no matter what he asked, you would say yes?

For a few years I knew God was calling me to some form of leadership in the church. I kept thinking I'd meet a lovely guy, get married and we'd lead together. As time rolled by the guy hadn't shown up but God was continually increasing my passion for his church. God challenged me that to be fully surrendered to him I just need to say 'Yes'. Not 'Yes, when this happens' or 'Yes, if that happens', just 'Yes'. I had to let go of the assumptions I'd made about my future and trust God that he knew best.

Sophie

The example of Jesus

Jesus gives us the ultimate example of what a surrendered heart looks like. As his death draws near we see this incredible portrait of a man who is 'overwhelmed with sorrow to the point of death' at the prospect of what God is asking him to do, but finds the strength to say he would rather do things God's way than his own: 'Father, if you are willing, take this cup from me; yet not my will, but yours be done' (Luke 22:42).

There's no arguing here, none of the bartering and rash promises we get tempted with. ('If you take this away from me, I will get up early and read the Bible for an hour every day for the rest of my life', etc.) There is an honesty about what Jesus wants, but a relinquishing of control to his Father by saying 'but what you want is more important than what I want'. Jesus knew he was loved. He knew God is good so he knew there was a good reason for God to send him to the cross. This helps us, when we face painful situations of our own, to remember Jesus knows that agony of submitting to the Father's ways, rather than choosing his own. It also reminds us we can still ask questions and be obedient. We don't have to pretend submitting to God's will is easy for us: but being surrendered means saying yes to God's ways.

A life surrendered to God

Many of us would prefer it if surrendering were a one-off thing. We could do it on the day we became a Christian and that would be it. Or if we only had to do it over big things that felt like huge steps of faith we could get excited about. But it doesn't work like that. As Pete Greig says in *God on Mute*:

. . . for most of us, laying down our lives rarely looks or feels heroic. Instead it takes the mundane form of a daily struggle, sacrificing ourselves not just once but repeatedly (Romans 12:1), preferring others, holding our tongues when we want to criticize and trusting God when we feel like quitting.[1]

God does ask us to surrender the big things in our lives: seeking him about what employment to take up; obeying his will when it comes to relationships; listening to see if he wants us to stay where we are or move to the other side of the world. These are the key choices in life which come along every so often, and we tend to pray about them and offer them to God. But what about the everyday choices? How will I treat my friends and family? How will I spend my money? How will I react when someone criticises me? Some of these are split second decisions but we have to be willing to go God's way in each and every one of them if we're to be fully submitted to his will. Think about whether these areas of your life are currently submitted to God:

- How you spend your time? Do you prioritise the things God wants, or do you think of your time as your own?
- How you spend your money? Do you tithe regularly, and try to live with a generous heart?
- Do you 'love your neighbour as yourself'?
- Is there somewhere or someone you turn to for comfort before God?
- Do you trust God with your future? Do you submit your hopes and dreams to him?

---

[1] P. Greig, *God on Mute* (Eastbourne: Kingsway, 2007), p. 212.

Letting go of fear

Fear can so often stop us from being fully open to God. It's easy for any of us who would hate to work in Africa to immediately think if we surrender to God, he will send us there, and never let us come home. Or, those of us who would love to pursue a musical career might think if we surrender to God, he'll send us to work in a church instead. Sometimes, God will ask us to do something we don't want to do, but, on the whole, he puts desires into our hearts for a reason. He's not cruel, he doesn't play with us and put a passion in our hearts for one thing, only to ask us to do something that is the complete opposite forever. God knows us far better than we know ourselves and he loves us more than we can imagine. Couldn't you trust someone like that to plan your future for you?

Fear can also trap us into worrying what other people will think of us. If we're serious about following God he may well ask us to do things that other people don't understand. We may feel like Noah as we build our ark and have people laughing at our craziness. However, if we're truly following after God then his opinion will be the most important to us and as long as we know we're doing what is right in his eyes, then we will be able to deal with having other people question us. We need to get to the place in our relationship with God where we love him so much that we couldn't conceive of not doing his will, no matter what the cost.

Counting the cost

There is a very real and serious challenge to us if we want to surrender to God. Jesus never pretended it would be easy and sometimes we can be in danger of watering it down because we don't want to put people off. The truth is Jesus warned us we should count the cost, and decide if we are willing to pay it, before we say yes to him:

> 'And anyone who does not carry his cross and follow me cannot be my disciple. Suppose one of you wants to build a tower. Will he not first sit down and estimate the cost to see if he has enough money to complete it? For if he lays the foundation and is not able to finish it, everyone who sees it will ridicule him, saying, "This fellow began to build and was not able to finish." . . . In the same way, any of you who does not give up everything he has cannot be my disciple.' (Luke 14:27–30,33)

This could sound like Jesus is being negative but he's asking us to take this seriously. He wants us to consider if we're really ready to let him take the reins of our lives. We have to remember Jesus doesn't want to take control in order to make us miserable. His desire for us is that we have life and have it to the full (John 10:10), and he knows the only way to do this is for us to surrender fully to him.

Jesus warned us we should count the cost.

This is why Jesus is saying we have to give up everything:

> 'Whoever finds his life will lose it, and whoever loses his life for my sake will find it.' (Matthew 10:39)

'I tell you the truth, unless a grain of wheat falls to the ground and dies, it remains only a single seed. But if it dies, it produces many seeds. The man who loves his life will lose it, while the man who hates his life in this world will keep it for eternal life.' (John 12:24–25)

At the heart of the Christian message is this: we must die to self to live in Christ. To truly be able to take up our cross, we have to have complete confidence in the fact that Jesus said he came to give us real life, and trust, in our loving Father. We have to know that he is kind, that he knows us, and that he wants to give us fullness of life, not rob us of joy. When we realise his goodness we can surrender everything in our lives to him, knowing he will make good on his promise that we will find life in him.

While I was on a discipleship course I had a very small amount of money; there was nothing spare for new clothes or meals out. I remember receiving my first paycheck after the course and, just as I was planning what I would spend it on, Tearfund launched an appeal in response to a drought in Pakistan which had left thousands of people malnourished and starving. I was reading a book called Rich Christians in an Age of Hunger and felt that God was asking me to bring my choices into line with his bias towards the poor. I also knew the parable of the widow's mite and felt that God was saying he was more concerned about what I kept than what I gave. I knew I had to give in a way that cost me something so, after I had taken care of the essentials, I gave the rest away and continued to try to keep living simply like I had been whilst I was on the discipleship course. I have learnt that although in the moment it can be painful to choose to say 'yes' to his ways and 'no' to mine, it often leads to a place of joy and peace that come from living out of obedience.

Sarah

Will I still mess up?

Sadly, while we live this side of heaven none of us is going to be perfect, which means we will keep messing up and sinning. So does that mean we're not fully surrendered? I don't think so. Once again, King David is a real inspiration for us whenever we find ourselves back in the place where we've sinned and got it wrong again. The Bible says of David that he was a man after God's own heart (1 Samuel 13:14), but we also read he committed adultery and had his lover's husband murdered – not exactly someone we would hold up as a shining example. The important thing for us to remember about David, when it comes to his sin, is that he didn't think 'I've blown it', and walk away. He turned back to God, faced his punishment and prayed for forgiveness. Because of Jesus we no longer suffer punishment for our sin (though we may, of course, have to deal with its consequences). We will mess up. But our God is a God of grace, who loves us and wants us to come back to him when we're shamefaced, not turn away.

- Are there any no-go areas of your life when it comes to God having control?
- What are your fears about saying yes to God?

- Do you feel like you have a right to certain things? When we're fully surrendered we accept all we have is a gift from God and he owes us nothing. We are indebted to him, not the other way around.
- Can you say along with Mother Theresa, 'God, there is nothing I won't do for you and whatever you ask I will do without delay'?

Many years ago I decided I would only marry a British guy! I had started travelling a lot through my job, and I think I got a bit scared that on one of my travels I might encounter a handsome foreign stranger, and I'd be forced to give up my home town and emigrate to some far-flung shore! So I told myself and anyone else who cared to listen I would never marry a foreigner. Then, about five years ago, God had a word with me. He really clearly told me to repent, he said, 'I don't want you to ever say "never" or "no" to me and that includes the specifics of who you will or will not marry.' I really hadn't thought through or realised that my attitude on the subject was not submissive to God, and I was genuinely sorry and told him so. I don't know if it was coincidence that four months later I met my very Australian husband. Regardless, it was a good lesson, one I have to learn and relearn over again, that to be fully submitted to God, open to his voice, and ready and willing to obey, we have to do away with our no-go areas, our exceptions and our reservations.

Ali

8

The Free Heart
(Ali)

I run in the path of your commands,
for you have set my heart free. (Psalm 119:32, TNIV)

Years ago I decided I was a failure. I didn't even realise I'd given myself that name at the time but everything I tried to do was coloured by the belief I was destined to mess up. It began with a situation at work where I was trying lots of new things and although there weren't any great disasters, the people around me didn't support me in my attempts. I put in more and more effort to try and get better results but each time I felt ripped apart. With hindsight, I can see that what I needed was someone to support me as I tried to develop but, instead, I got laughed at. Each time we had a team meeting, I would walk home crying and feeling humiliated. Day by day, my confidence was eroded, and I felt like nothing I brought to that workplace was good enough.

It hurt me so much that, when I left that job, I sat in my car and told God it had been the worst time in my life, I was never going to think about it again and I was never going to go near any of the gifts I had tried so unsuccessfully to use in that place. So I began a new job, without dealing with any of that pain in my heart, and threw my all into my new role. I worked myself into the ground, literally to the point where I was incredibly sick and couldn't carry on. That just reaffirmed in my mind that I was a failure and everything I tried to do would fail.

Because I believed in my heart I was a failure, I couldn't accept the things God was calling me to. He spoke to me clearly, over a long period of time, about stepping up into leadership but I couldn't do it, I was too frightened. How could God trust me with anything if I was only going to fail and let him down? Like Moses, I had lots of conversations with God along the lines of 'Get someone else to do it.' Then, one day, I was reading through my old journals, and I saw just how many times God had spoken to me and I had ignored it. I was gutted to see how disobedient I had been and I cried my eyes out. I had never faced up to the root of my feelings of failure, never dealt with the mistakes I had made, nor forgiven the people who made me feel like I'd failed when I hadn't. I had thought I was justified in telling God I was no good for the job, but, in answering God back and ignoring him, I was just being disobedient and missing out on so many good things he had for me.

I don't think it's just me either. Lots of us get caught up in things that have happened to us and we can let them define who we are. Sometimes, we have to stop and think about who we actually believe we are in

We have to question whether we're defined by the past, or whether our hearts and our minds are free.

our hearts. We have to question whether we're defined by the past, or whether our hearts and our minds are free.

For some of us, it's not just experiences that have caused us to believe negative things about ourselves, we've also had people tell us things like we're not good, we're not wanted, we're ugly, we're stupid, we're unloved or we're unlovable. Words like this wound us deeply, especially when they come from someone we look up to, love and respect. Likewise, if we've had a situation recur in our lives we can start to believe we're abandoned, we're a victim or we're a failure.

If we believe these things deep down, then our actions will echo our thoughts. We're trapped because we find it hard to hear and respond to God's truth when we've surrendered to our negative feelings. In the Bible, Gideon is a classic example of this. When God called him to save Israel from the Midians, Gideon couldn't see it happening and he replied: 'How can I save Israel? My clan is the weakest in Manasseh, and I am the least in my family' (Judges 6:15). Gideon struggled to respond to God's call initially because he was trapped by his past and his circumstances. He saw himself as weak and he didn't understand why God would want to use him or believe God could.

Sometimes, the impact on us is more simple: if we were treated as a nuisance by the people who looked after us as a child, we may battle to believe God is interested in us and find it hard to bring everything to God in prayer for fear of annoying him. If we've never been shown grace by those around us and have been punished severely for our actions, we may see ourselves only as 'sinner' and find it hard to accept God's forgiveness and grace.

God knows the truth of who we are. He wants to take the negative things we have picked up along the way and reshape our view of ourselves. He wants to heal us of our pain by giving us free hearts not bound by lies. He wants to take the negative names we have acquired for ourselves and give us a new name and a new identity.

For my dissertation I had to do some in-depth interviews which I recorded and then transcribed. After each interview I'd think, 'Oh, that wasn't very good; I'm no good at this; I bet they thought I was wasting their time,' along with a whole lot of other negative things about myself. However, when it came to typing them up and listening to them, I was pleasantly surprised. It really wasn't that bad; I'd asked some good questions and managed to keep the interviews on track. It made me realise that I have never truthfully thought I am any good at anything. I'm 'OK', maybe, but not 'good', particularly when it comes to dealing with people, even though I love it. I traced it back to my school days when I was a loner and excluded from the main friendship groups. God showed me the experience had left me with a filter through which I was viewing my whole life, including my relationships with people. The filter was wrong, so how I felt about conversations and my interpretation was incorrect: in fact, it was quite far off. I've prayed about it since, and really asked the Lord to show me whenever that old filter kicks in, as it's something I slip back into occasionally. Learning this about myself was perhaps one of the most valuable things I learnt through doing the dissertation!

Juliet

Who does the Bible say I am?

When we're trying to work out who we are, the first place to go for truth is the Bible and here we see some things that God says are true of all his children. When we pick them out of God's word we begin to get a picture of who we are in our Father's eyes. These words are so vital for us to truly shape our identity in Jesus and not in the world. We can come back to them time and time again to understand how God sees us, and to allow the truth of them to take root in our hearts and shape our minds.

- The whole Bible tells us we're loved but John 3:16 specifically tells us God loved us so much he was willing to send his son to die for us. Romans 8:38–39 assures us there's absolutely nothing that can separate us from this love.
- Genesis 1:27 tells us we are made in God's image and verse 31 says when he made us he saw his work was 'very good'.
- 1 Peter 2:9 says we are chosen and belong to God.
- Romans 8:16–17 says we are God's children and his heirs.
- We are forgiven. Ephesians 1:7 says it's through Jesus, through his grace and the blood he shed on the cross that our sins are forgiven – not by anything we've done.
- We also know from 1 Corinthians 13 that love 'keeps no record of wrongs' which means not only have we been forgiven, but that our past is not held against us.
- Matthew 10:29–31 tells us that we're valuable: 'Are not two sparrows sold for a penny? Yet not one of them will fall to the ground apart from the will of

your Father. And even the very hairs of your head are all numbered. So don't be afraid; you are worth more than many sparrows.'

- John 15 talks about us being friends of God.
- Zephaniah 3:17 says God 'will take great delight in you, he will quiet you with his love, he will rejoice over you with singing.'
- John 8:36 says we are free: 'So if the Son sets you free, you will be free indeed.'
- We are his – Isaiah 43:1 says, 'Fear not . . . I have summoned you by name; you are mine.'

These are just some of the amazing things the Bible tells us about who we are in God. This is the truth we need to get to grips with and cling to. So many of us, in different areas of our lives, get used to listening to the lies but John 8:32 says, when we know the truth, that truth will set us free.

Read these statements and think about whether you believe them in your heart:

- You are chosen by God, therefore you haven't been forgotten.
- You are God's child, therefore you are not a mistake.
- You are made in God's image, therefore all the bad things you believe about yourself just can't be true.
- You are loved, not rejected.
- You have sinned, but you are forgiven and not condemned.
- You are valuable, not worthless.
- You are a friend of God, not just a servant.
- You're known by God; you're not just a face in the crowd.
- God takes delight in you; you're not a burden to him, or something he just tolerates.

- You are free; which means you are not a slave to sin, or to what others say you are or you aren't.
- You are God's, therefore you have nothing to fear.

Do you see that we give ourselves names such as 'worthless', 'sinner' and 'unloved', but God is whispering something completely different in our ear? We're going round with name tags emblazoned with things like 'abandoned' and God is saying our badge should say 'chosen'. To experience a free heart we have to get these truths embedded in our heads and our hearts. We have to know who God says we are so that we can stand against the lies and see them for what they are. The truth of who God says we are will set us free so read and re-read the things God says about you: pray about them; recognise the things you struggle to believe; and put them on your wall so you can see them every day. Ask God to show you the truth about who you actually are so that you might live in his freedom.

I used to feel forgotten and over-looked, and although God kept speaking to me and telling me he saw me and knew me, I could never quite believe it in my heart. One morning at church I was being prayed for and God told me that if I continued to believe he overlooked me, I was actually sinning. It's not possible for him to forget his children (Isaiah 49:15) and to say that he did was not only wrong, but offensive to his character. I knew from that moment on that I had to trust in who God said I was, trust in his amazing love, and let go of the things I used to believe about myself.

Jane

Named by God

As well as all the amazing things God says about us all, there are also specific things that he speaks over us as individuals. They help us understand the things he has called us to and, when he gives them to us, we need to listen. We

We have to trust God made us so he knows what we're made for.

might not always think the name fits straightaway, but we have to trust God made us so he knows what we're made for. He knows how he can use us, no matter what we might think, or what the circumstances might be.

Earlier, I mentioned how Gideon responded when God called him to save the Israelites. He saw his own weakness and didn't want to step up to the plate. But what I didn't say was that when God met with Gideon the first thing he did was call him a mighty warrior. It's confusing to understand this given Gideon's less than warrior-like attitude, but that is what God said! In fact, God made a habit of giving people names others might not have. God changed Abram's name to Abraham which means father of many. It didn't seem to bother him that Abraham and Sarah were struggling to conceive at the time. How about Simon Peter? He was the one Jesus called 'the rock' but when we look at the gospels we don't exactly see rock-like behaviour from him. I'd say he was a bit more of an 'open your mouth and speak before you've engaged your brain' type. Remember the story of Jesus' transfiguration? It's one of the most incredible stories in the gospels and worth reading in full in Matthew 17. To paraphrase: Jesus took Peter, James and John up a mountain. Jesus started glowing, his clothes turned whiter than Daz white and the long dead Moses and Elijah turned up for a chat. Peter said, 'Lord, it is good for us to be here. If you wish, I will put up three shelters – one for you, one for Moses and one for Elijah.' Talk about killing the moment. I'm definitely someone who could be described as talking a lot, some would say too much. But I don't reckon even I would have responded to the trans-figuration like Peter did.

Then there's the Garden of Gethsemane, when Peter couldn't keep his eyes open even for an hour or two. This is quickly followed by the slightly awkward moment at Jesus' arrest when he cuts the ear off a servant. And then his *pièce-de-résistance*: the well-docu-mented denial of Jesus. To be honest, reading about Peter is the one thing that makes me so glad I wasn't around in Jesus' time. Could you imagine if there was always someone around to record all of your most embarrassing and ditsy moments for people to study centuries on? Properly traumatic.

It's easy to look at these things and wonder what Jesus was talking about when he called Peter 'the rock'. But, then we remember he was the only disciple who got out of the boat to go to Jesus when he was walking on water. We can call it lack of faith that he started to sink but how about giving him some credit for having enough faith to get out of the boat in the first place? His courage and desire to be doing the amazing things Jesus was doing gives us an idea of what Jesus saw in him.

When others turned their back on Jesus we read in John: '"You do not want to leave too, do you?" Jesus asked the Twelve. Simon Peter answered him, "Lord, to whom shall we go? You have the words of eternal life. We believe and know that you are the Holy One of God."' (6:67–69).

Then there's the time when Jesus washes the disciples' feet (John 13). Peter refuses at first, not wanting Jesus to take the role of a servant for him. When Jesus explains, 'Unless I wash you, you have no part with me', Peter throws himself in with typical enthusiasm saying, in that case, wash my feet, my hands and my head as well! I love that so much. Yes, Peter made mistakes, was hot-headed and put his foot in it, but somewhere in there we get a glimpse of how God saw him.

When we read the rest of the New Testament we learn that after Jesus ascended, Peter was someone who would preach the gospel and see thousands of people coming to know God. Not only that, in Acts 15 we see Peter giving wise and reasoned advice to the early church, communicating God's truth to the rest of the council and truly being 'the rock' of the church. Peter could have looked at himself and said, 'I'm a failure. I don't know when to keep my mouth shut, I'm always in the way, causing trouble or embarrassing myself. God can't use me.' But he saw past the mistakes he'd made, and the ways his enthusiasm had created a stir, and he gave himself fully to God to use.

All along, God was right. God knew Peter was the rock even when no one else could see it. Should we be surprised at that? God called Gideon a warrior when he was weak and afraid, he called Abraham a father of nations when he was childless, and Peter a rock when he was anything but.

What is God saying to you? Who does he say you are? Maybe you've struggled to hear the positive things he's said because your heart has been trapped by lies that have been spoken to you, or circumstances that have hurt you. Ask God to give you a free heart able to respond to his truth and his ways. Ask him to speak to you about the particular names he's given you. They might relate to your calling such as evangelist, teacher, friend, leader, pioneer, prophet, mother, mentor, musician, artist, entrepreneur, youth worker or politician. Or, he might want to say something about your character and call you joyful, kind, gracious, beautiful, loving, tender-hearted, faithful, loyal or peaceful. There are so many things God will call us to and things he will say about our character, if we will only listen. We need to learn to let go of our past and not to listen to the things that would hold us back like our circumstances, insecurities and brokenness. Only then will we be free and able to respond to God as he speaks his truth into our lives.

I found my first three years of secondary school hard, I didn't seem to fit in that well and I was bullied. I was hurt and I started taking it out on my other relationships. I started to push people out of my life, and I didn't trust the people who cared about me. I became lonely and labelled myself as 'unlovable'. I had known about the story of Jesus and the idea of a loving God, but I never believed it, how could God love the unlovable? I never thought God could come and meet me and love me, but he did. When I first met with the Holy Spirit I didn't know what was going on, but all I felt was joy and love. Because of God's love I've started to let people in and not push them away. I've made amazing new friends and I love that I get to be a part of their journey. God's given me a wonderful loving family at my church and he definitely doesn't label me as unlovable – he calls me 'beloved'.

Nathalie

9

The Resurrected Heart
(Ali)

You who seek God, inquiring for and requiring Him [as
your first need], let your hearts revive and live!
(Psalms 69:32, Amplified Bible)

Throughout this book we've been looking at how we
examine our hearts and seeing some of the ways they
need healing and changing before God. But, what happens if you feel like your heart has been too greatly damaged for you to trust or hope in God? What do you do if
you realise your heart is hard but you're too scared to
soften it? What about if you feel you've been satisfying
your heart in the wrong ways but you don't know how
to come back to God? If you've been particularly badly
hurt, or been wounded over a consistent period of time,
it may feel like something in your heart has died. Maybe
it's a small part of your heart that feels it has been damaged, or maybe you feel as though the whole thing has
been trampled, bruised and broken beyond all recognition. For some of us, life has been so hard that we buried
our hearts a while back, they've become numb and we
don't know how to reconnect to God. If any of these

situations rings a bell in your life, what happens next? Is there a way to reverse the damage? Is there any hope of restoration?

There's a story in John's gospel (chapter 11) that gives us a resounding yes. It's the story of Lazarus and you might be familiar with it, so I'll recap it briefly: Lazarus got sick, his sisters (Mary and Martha, who were good friends of Jesus) asked Jesus to come to them. Jesus stayed where he was for two more days, and by the time he arrived, Lazarus was dead.

If you know the story, you know how it ends, but let's pause here and remember Mary and Martha didn't have the advantage of fast-forwarding to the good bit, just as we don't get to skip ahead to see what's coming in our lives. As far as Mary and Martha were concerned the situation was bleak. They'd spent days worrying about their sick brother, they sent for Jesus knowing he could heal Lazarus and bring comfort to them, but he didn't reach them and their brother died. Imagine how painful that was. Think about what sort of thoughts might have been going through their heads. Why didn't Jesus come sooner? How could he let Lazarus die? Did he ever truly love us like we thought? His absence may have felt like it spoke volumes to them: it says it all. You don't stay away when people you love are sick and hurting, and you are in a position to do something about it. Mary and Martha may have questioned whether they'd completely misjudged who Jesus was and how much he cared about them. Mary, who anointed Jesus with oil, may have been tempted to ask if her devotion, her service, and her worship to God meant nothing.

When bad things happen to us we often want to ask why God would let such a thing take place. If he's God and he's in control, why would he let that person die, leave us or hurt us so badly? Why did he let us fall flat on our face when we tried to take a step of faith? Why didn't he protect us better? Rather than healing our hearts after they're broken, why didn't he just keep them whole in the first place? Part of what we're asking when we're in this pain is, 'God, do you really love me?' The answer for us is the same as it was for Mary and Martha – a resounding yes. The truth is we can't look at our personal circumstances as proof of whether or not God loves us. The cross is the only place we need to look to know how God feels:

> This is how God showed his love among us: He sent his one and only Son into the world that we might live through him. This is love: not that we loved God, but that he loved us and sent his Son as an atoning sacrifice for our sins. (1 John 4:9–10)

Circumstances change, good and bad things come our way, but God is constant and unchanging – his love for us never wavers.

Of course, Mary and Martha didn't know about the cross at that point but we know from reading John 11:5 that Jesus *did* love the sisters and Lazarus. His love for them wasn't the issue, so what was going on when he didn't go to them immediately? We have to remember there is a perspective we can't see. The cross looked like the most enormous failure on Good Friday. Joseph's life looked like it was in ruins as he languished in jail. Job's friends all thought his sin was the

The cross looked like the most enormous failure on Good Friday.

reason for his suffering. God's ways are not our ways. He doesn't do things as we expect and he can use *all* things for good. Sometimes we see good come out of a bad situation and we understand a little bit of why things happened the way they did. But often those 'why' questions don't get answered, and we have to hold on to the fact that whatever situations we find ourselves in, God loves us and he always will.

Jesus loved the family in this story so much but he chose not to rush to them. Why? To bring God glory. His response on hearing of Lazarus's illness was, 'This sickness will not end in death. No, it is for God's glory so that God's Son may be glorified through it' (John 11:4).

But that doesn't mean Jesus was hardened to Mary and Martha's suffering. The Bible tells us when Jesus saw Mary crying he was 'deeply moved' (v. 33) and he himself wept (v. 35). In the same way, I don't believe he says to us, 'Just deal with it, it's for my glory.' When we're upset, he feels our pain, when people hurt us, it hurts him. He's deeply moved by the things that have happened to you.

As Mary, Martha and those around them mourn, they notice Jesus crying and they understand how much he loved Lazarus. They vocalise what we sometimes want to ask in our similar situations: could the man who healed a blind man not have changed this situation too? Jesus chose to allow Lazarus to die but as we read on we know he went on to do something quite incredible. Jesus stood before the tomb and he called Lazarus out. The man may have been dead for four days but Jesus simply said, 'Lazarus, come out!' and out he walked. Jesus raised Lazarus back to life. He called out to him and restored what had been taken from him. Today, Jesus is calling us out too. He's calling us out from the tombs we've found ourselves in: the graves that represent the places of hopelessness and despair in our lives; the tombs that show where our dreams have died; and the places where we have retreated so that no one can reach us and we can be 'safe'.

Jesus calls us out:

- Where we have died little deaths over disappointment, pain and heartache – he calls us out.
- Where fear of rejection or failure has kept us hidden, and we've chosen self-protection instead of faith or hope – he calls us out.
- Where a hope deferred has made us sick and something inside has died – he calls us out.
- Where we have trusted someone, been hurt and closed down our heart – he calls us out.
- Where we've hardened our hearts because of pain and disappointment – he calls us out.

He calls us out because although it's neat and tidy in the graveyard, and we think we'll never get hurt there, there's no life there either. And Jesus came not just to give us life, but life in abundance.

Many of us need God to wake up our hearts again. We need to allow him to call us out of the tombs we've found ourselves in and bring us to a place of life and joy again. Our Saviour who was himself resurrected, longs to resurrect our hearts, our dreams, our hopes and our faith. He wakes us up and calls us out, *Come forth, come forward, come out of hiding, leave your places of self protection and disappointment*. He calls us into his light, into his healing and freedom where we allow ourselves to be seen again, where we allow him to work in us and use us. He wants to take us to a place where we give him free reign in our lives once again; a place where we are able to offer to him and to others who we *really* are.

For some of us, this feels scary: the idea of giving Jesus permission to work in our lives, to heal us and free us, sounds like it could be a bit messy and possibly even painful. When Jesus asked for the stone covering the tomb to be taken away, Martha objected that it would smell horribly. And she would have been right. A body decaying for four days? Not a good scent. Death stinks! I remember a few years ago I had to drive past the same spot each day where there was a dead badger at the side of the road. Though it was one of those beautiful spells of summery weather I had to keep my window tightly shut to save myself from gagging at the smell. Each day it got worse and worse. Now imagine that was a human body, trapped in a tomb in the Middle Eastern warmth. Then the stone blocking it in is removed. It would be disgusting. Martha knew that and was horrified at the idea, but Jesus wasn't fazed. He didn't say it wouldn't smell but simply said, 'Did I not tell you that if you believed, you would see the glory of God?'

We can't be afraid of the odour if we want to see the glory of God. Honestly? It will probably be a bit messy when we let Jesus roll away the stone. When we let out pain there is usually a fair amount of tears; it can be quite uncomfortable and, depending on how badly we've been hurt, the process of healing isn't usually one quick fix. But all that mess is already inside us. Ignoring it doesn't make it go away. The only way we can be rid of it is to let it be released, messy or not. So, like Lazarus, we need to hear and respond to Jesus' call. And we need to allow him to not just wake us up and call us out of our tombs, but to take our grave clothes off too. John tells us when Lazarus came out his hands and feet were wrapped with strips of linen and there was a cloth around his face (v. 44). Jesus commanded these be removed and it's obvious why. It's possible to be alive, but stuck and bound by the trappings of the grave. If Lazarus had stayed as he was, with those grave clothes in place, they would have restricted what he could do and say. There would have been no freedom.

God doesn't just call us out of our grave: he also longs to remove the things that have bound us like fear, negative thought patterns, vows, sin and intimidation. Freedom is not just about being called out of darkness, it's about cutting off the chains, and this is what Jesus came to do. He came to bring release to the captives (Isaiah 61:1). He wants us to be free to hear his voice, to feel his heart and to follow where he calls.

Jesus came to give us life in all its fullness, a free life – not hindered nor held back by a hard heart or an enslaved mind, sorrow over our past or fear of our future, nor over patterns of behaviour or thought. There's a hymn I love which declares it powerfully:

> My chains fell off, my heart was free,
> I rose, went forth and followed thee![1]

It seems to perfectly express this freedom God has in mind for us. It's not down to us to break our own chains and find our own way to freedom – God does it for us. He is the giver of life. Our job is to say yes – to allow him into the places in our heart that are anxious, hurt and afraid. We start the process of healing simply by saying yes to God, and giving him permission to call us out of the grave and remove our grave clothes. He may bring us healing as we meet with him in worship or in prayer. He might heal us through friendships, relationships or counselling. He may renew our hearts and minds as we read his word. Often, he uses a combination of so many

---

[1] Charles Wesley, 'And can it be'.

different things to heal us, sometimes it's obvious, and sometimes we can barely see it's happening until we look back and see how much we've changed. One thing we don't have to worry about though is whether he wants to. God cares so passionately about your heart. He wants it to be a heart that is free and is fully alive.

When I was sixteen, my sports coach of four years made an attempt to sexually abuse me. I had trusted him with my life; he was like a granddad to me and to learn that he had been grooming me, the whole time I'd known him, just broke me. I felt scared, abandoned and sick to my stomach at the thought of him. My head said it was no one's fault but his, but in my heart I was angry towards everyone. How had they let me suffer? I was constantly scared that he would try to snatch me and everything reminded me of him. It was around this time too that my parents split up and my older sister left for uni. I felt like nothing in my life was under my control. So I decided to regain control where I could by doing what I wanted, when I wanted. Subconsciously, I think I really wanted to hurt my mum and dad. I forgot about God in an instant and started drinking, going out late and getting more involved with guys. I became increasingly angry, bitter, resistant and uncontrollable. I wanted things my way. I wanted to take back the control I felt the coach had taken from me. I hated how I looked so I changed, and I hated anyone who opposed me or went against what I wanted. My heart had died, and was replaced by anger, hurt and hate. What I didn't realise was that throughout the entire time, my mum had been praying for me that I would see God's love again. And with help from God, mentors and my family, I was drawn out of the world I had created and into God's arms again. It took a long time of learning to forgive, and learning what real love was like, but I was restored and my heart was pieced back together bit by bit with every affirming word, prayer and act of love.

Lahna

Rachel's story

'You can do what you like. You can say what you like. You can hit me as hard as you want to. But I won't cry. I won't let you win.'

I think I must have been around ten years old when I made that statement. I can certainly picture the scene in my head; it's one of the strongest childhood memories I have. My mum was sitting on the sofa and I was standing in front of her, being told off yet again for ruining her life by 'being born'. In many ways, this was just another average day in my childhood. Except it wasn't. It was the day when everything changed. It was the day I decided, finally, that allowing my heart to feel wasn't working for me anymore. And from that moment on, I was tougher. Stronger. Better. This was me against the world. I was determined I wasn't going to lose any more. No one would ever make me cry.

Ten-year-old children don't get to that point easily, and I've often wondered why I didn't ask someone for help. I think a big part of the reason I didn't say anything was because I genuinely believed what my mum told me was true: I deserved to be hit and abused. My being born was the worst thing that had ever happened to her, and there was nothing I could do to make it better. The best thing to do was to keep out of the way, stay out of trouble, and work out how to avoid making the situation worse.

Less than a year after I made my vow to be strong, my dad began to spend more time away from our family home, and he continued to do so over the next seven years. My mum had always been careful to 'leave me alone' when my dad was around, so his increasing absence left the door open for her to be much freer in doing and saying whatever she wanted to. This inevitably meant that the abuse got worse. It also meant that the cracks in my mum's own emotional health began to become more pronounced.

Even though I'd seen it coming, I was still surprised when my dad told me he'd been having an affair with someone and was leaving for good. Within a few weeks of my dad's leaving, my mum's depression and suicidal threats increased to the point she was admitted to a psychiatric hospital. I was eighteen years old, my brother was sixteen, and my younger sister was twelve. For the next year or so, I attempted to fill the role of parent. I went to parents' evenings, shopped for food, washed clothes, and paid the domestic bills. This was no time to cry or to show weakness. From the outside looking in, it may have looked like we were surviving well. But things were anything but OK.

One of the things I found most difficult during my teenage years was the unpredictability of life. Sometimes I'd come home and things seemed calm. Other days I'd walk through the door and Mum would scream at me, threatening to kill me because she'd heard a rumour I'd met Dad for lunch. The way I learnt to cope was to plan for the worst. That way, if the worst happened, I would be ready for it. I shut out of my mind any positive expectation or hope. I was too afraid of being disappointed.

As a result, I completely lost the ability to relax, and I was always anxious. As soon as I was old enough to buy alcohol, I began to use it as a crutch. Though I didn't drink vast amounts, it wasn't long before the only way I could get to sleep was to drink before bedtime. My mum blamed me for her mental health issues and I took her words to heart, fully believing it was my fault she was ill. I had no idea what to do with that shame and guilt. The only way I thought I could get rid of my bad feelings was to inflict punishment upon myself, either by injuring my body or by severely limiting my food intake. For a short time after I self-harmed, I would feel better. It was as if by making myself pay for being a 'bad child' I had gone some way towards righting a wrong. Later on, I'd often feel even more guilt for damaging my body, but I kept doing it because my heart was so desperate for even just a few minutes of feeling better.

Finally, my mum came out of hospital, and I left home to go to university. I remember leaving with the strong conviction life would be OK now. I was moving away from the place of abuse, so why wouldn't it be? I had no idea then it would take me another fourteen years to begin to find freedom.

I first became interested in the person of Jesus when I was about fifteen. Though my family didn't attend church, a local congregation asked me if I would come and play the piano for them. That led to me going on a youth group weekend away where I was really struck by how relaxed and fun the speakers were. In contrast to anything I'd experienced, these people seemed to have a freedom and joy for life that was captivating. Over the course of the weekend, they kept telling us Jesus was the source of freedom. That caught my attention.

After the weekend, I decided to investigate for myself. So I read the Bible. All the way through. Twice. I worked hard to understand who Jesus was. Eventually, I was convinced that the Bible was true. I resolved to make Christianity the foundation of my life.

I tried hard to earn God's love. I worked for Christian charities. I tried to help the poor. I read my Bible regularly, went to church, and tried to be nice. In some ways, life did get a little better. I was away from the daily trials I'd faced growing up, but I certainly hadn't found the freedom and joy that had attracted me to learn about Jesus in the first place.

I began to notice other Christians who spoke a different language to me. One I couldn't understand. It wasn't that they used complex theological terms, but they talked as if they actually had a relationship with God. They seemed to believe he loved them unconditionally and felt free to say that they loved him in return. With the vow I made as a ten year old still firmly in place, I had no box where I could put this kind of language. I'd never heard anyone say that they loved me. I had no idea what love might feel like.

Over time, I began to explore my emotions a little. But rather than finding freedom, I just got frustrated, then angry, and, in the end, guilty. I could usually understand complex concepts quickly; why was understanding emotions so difficult? I just couldn't make myself feel. It was as if my heart were dead, and there was nothing I could do to make it come alive.

One day, things began to change. I was giving a friend a lift home from the office, and she told me about a time when she'd wrestled with God over never having had a daughter. As I went to bed that night, it suddenly struck me that I'd never had a mum, at least not a nurturing, loving parent. That night, my heart began to feel. The tears, left unshed for years, finally began to flow. It frightened me; I felt like I might never stop crying.

Over the next few weeks, as I chatted with my friend about what was happening, she suggested we pray with someone together. This was the last thing I wanted to do! I hated being the centre of attention and the idea of sitting with two other people to pray about my heart was not something I was keen on. But I was desperate for change, so, reluctantly, I agreed to go.

At the beginning of the prayer time, they explained we'd be praying through some of the significant events of my life and asking Jesus if there was anything he'd like to say to me about them. As much as I thought they were nice people, this suggestion seemed a little crazy. I figured it was appropriate to let them know I didn't generally (as in, *ever!*) hear Jesus talking to me personally, so we should set our expectations fairly low. This didn't seem to put them off, and we began to pray. As we did, somewhat hesitantly, I actually did begin to hear Jesus speaking to me. When they suggested we meet again to pray, my earlier reluctance was replaced by a sense of anticipation and, over the next few months, my heart began to come alive. Jesus gently encouraged me to give up the vows I had made as a ten year old and to repent of the pride I was holding in my heart. I confessed to him, with my friends as witnesses, the ways in which I'd damaged my body. I asked him to give me the strength and courage to forgive those who had hurt me and to let him walk me towards a new life and a new day in him.

It wasn't easy. A resurrected heart can feel, and feeling pain and letting tears fall was something I'd been avoiding my whole life. But though it felt hard, it also felt right, and things began to change very quickly. As my heart learnt to feel, it also began to hope. It began to believe things could get better. It began to see that life in relationship with God, and with others, is actually better than a life of self-protected isolation. Above all, I began to realise healing wasn't something I had to work out logically in my head, rather it was something I had to allow Jesus to bring to my resurrected heart.

I'm now ten months on from that prayer session, and it wouldn't be an exaggeration to say that my whole view of life has changed. I'm still working out loads of things, but at least I'm now heading in the right direction. And I'm continuing to learn, over and over again, that change happens not when I force it to, but when I allow Jesus to help me walk in freedom with him.

One day, I understood his love, acceptance and forgiveness very clearly when he brought back to my mind an experience I'd had several years before. I had been involved with a charity which worked with children at risk in the developing world. As part of a promotional tour, the charity had flown over a teenager, Oscar, from South America, who they'd been helping for a number of years. Having visited churches across the UK telling his own story, it was time for Oscar to return home, and I was asked to accompany him on the long flights to ensure he made it safely back.

Oscar had been thrown out of home when he was just seven years old and had made his home on the edge of a large rubbish dump. Befriended by some charity workers, Oscar eventually agreed to move into one of their small, family-style children's homes. I'd known Oscar for a number of years, so it was a privilege to travel with him. He was an extremely easy kid to be around: well behaved, positive and with a cheeky sense of humour.

Two long flights later, we arrived at our destination. By this time, Oscar had somewhat lost his joy for life! He was tired, hungry, and not in the mood for a conversation. We stood quietly waiting for our suitcases to arrive and walked towards the exit. As we approached the main doors, we suddenly heard lots of clapping, shouting, and cheering from the balcony overhead. To our surprise, gathered together at the front of the balcony were the other boys from Oscar's home, along with the staff who cared for them, holding banners saying, 'Welcome home, Oscar. We missed you, Oscar!'

As soon as Oscar saw them, he suddenly brightened up. He turned to me with a wide smile and said, 'Rachel, look! I've got a family now, and they've come to pick me up from the airport.' He abandoned his suitcase with me and ran to greet his family. He knew he was back in a safe place with people who loved him and accepted him just as he was.

Ten months ago, as I began listening to Jesus speak to me, he helped me to see how this experience with Oscar was a brilliant picture of what he was offering to me now. For so many years, I had been doing the equivalent of walking through an airport, feeling tired, dragging a heavy suitcase behind me, not prepared to give up my pride and independence. I had known that things weren't right, but it had felt safer to live with the pain of what I knew, rather than to believe or hope things could be different.

Even though I hadn't been aware of it, throughout this time Jesus had been standing on the balcony, calling my name, holding a banner saying 'Welcome home' and waiting for me to run to him. Only he could sort out the suitcase of guilt, shame, pain, hurt, and disappointment I had collected over the years. And only he could bring healing to my heart, and help me to find security in living life with him.

The initial healing of my heart began as I abandoned my suitcase and ran to him for the first time. But that was just the start of the journey of living in freedom.

What I'm now learning is that every day, every morning, every evening, every time I need it, Jesus is still standing there on that balcony, waiting to take the suitcase of pain and ready to offer healing, love, forgiveness, and hope. All I have to do is to run to him.

If your heart is in need of his healing today, know that you too can abandon your suitcase and run to him. He also has a banner with your name on. And he's calling you to run to him.

Final word

The work on our hearts is something that will continue for the rest of our lives. Life is always changing, throwing us curve balls and putting different pressures on us. The quicker we are to recognise what is going on, and bring our hearts before God for his healing, the easier it becomes to keep them in line with how God wants them to be. We need to regularly ask the Holy Spirit to search our hearts and reveal to us any areas that need changing. This may help you as a little checklist for now or for the future.

- Are you aware of your outward behaviour and what it says about what's happening in your heart? When your reaction to a situation is extreme do you ask God to show you what's really going on?
- Are there areas where you're struggling to trust God at the moment? What truth can you draw on to remind you of God's character and promises?
- Are you anxious and in need of God's peace? Take some time to bring the significant and the insignificant things that are worrying you to your loving Father. Ask him to reveal any lies in your heart stopping you being at peace.

- Is there any area of your heart that has been hardened? Painful things can often make us shut down parts of our hearts which causes separation between us and God. Ask him to soften your heart again and heal the pain you've felt.
- Where do you look for satisfaction before you turn to God? Are you aware of the signs that your heart is hungry and in need of filling? Is there anything you need to walk away or fast from for a while to bring your focus back on God?
- Is your heart hopeful about the future? Are there areas where God is asking you to have hope in the face of difficult circumstances or where you are struggling to believe things could really change? Ask God to help you keep your hope in him and to deal with the pain of unmet hopes.
- Is your heart fully surrendered to God? Could he ask you to do anything and you'd say yes? Can you pray along with Jesus 'not my will, but yours be done'? Bring any situations or attitudes you find hard to surrender to God before him now and ask him to help you choose his ways, knowing he wants the best for you.
- Do you know who God says you are? Is your heart free to believe that or are there any lies in your heart you need to let go of?
- Are there any parts of your heart that have died through pain and disappointment? Ask God to resurrect your heart and to make you completely alive in him. Consider seeing a counsellor or praying through any particularly painful areas with a friend or church pastor.

Maybe some of these things are key issues in your life, maybe just small everyday concerns – but, no matter what the state of our hearts, there is always hope in God. Let's count on the very nature and character of our God and his desire to heal us. As Paul says: 'If God didn't hesitate to put everything on the line for us, embracing our condition and exposing himself to the worst by sending his own Son, is there anything else he wouldn't gladly and freely do for us?' (Romans 8:31–32, The Message). God's desire is we have fullness of life so every time we pray the words of King David that God would 'create', 'renew' and 'restore' (Psalms 51:10–12) our hearts, we know we are praying in his will. No matter how badly we've had our hearts damaged, he *can* heal us. He *wants* to heal us. He *longs* to heal us because he wants our hearts to be fully alive and fully his.

> Search me, O God, and know my heart;
> test me and know my anxious thoughts.
> See if there is any offensive way in me,
> and lead me in the way everlasting. (Psalms 139:23–24)

Acknowledgments

We would like to thank:

Everyone who read the manuscript for us, especially Jo Stockdale for going through it so thoroughly, and Jo Littledyke for her encouragement.

Those who shared their stories with us, particularly Jo, Kat and Rachel.

Mark Finnie and the team at Authentic.

And the incredible people in our lives who have helped shape and look after our hearts. You know who you are and you know we love you!

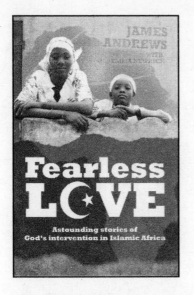

Fearless Love

Astounding stories of God's intervention in Islamic Africa

*James Andrews
with
Emma Newrick*

The Bible college you can read about in *Fearless Love* is based in a city in northern Nigeria, in the vicinity of the huge Islamic 'harvest field' of the African Sahel, just south of the Sahara desert. Until recent years the city had seen less killing of Christians than regions nearby. The founding team believed it would be a safe hub in which to train those God calls from the surrounding regions and nations to spread the gospel far and wide. However, as this city is a centre of gospel outreach the Islamic community is also aware of its strategic importance . . .

Fearless Love is a deeply challenging and informative book that tells the story of the college's mission to reach people with the gospel in the midst of Islamic jihad – in a hostile region where being a Christian, and especially converting to Christianity, may easily cost you your life.

978-1-85078-982-6

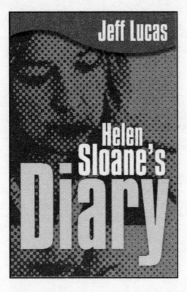

Helen Sloane's Diary

Jeff Lucas

Take Helen, a frustrated 27-year-old rookie social worker. Add Hayley, the world's worst teenager, Kristian,
the blond blue-eyed worship leader, faithful friend
James, old flame Aaron, corruption, chaos and passion
. . . and you've got *Helen Sloane's Diary*.

Blend in a New Age mother, a super-spiritual friend,
two deeply unpleasant church members and a personal
tragedy, as well as laughter, tears and thought-provok-
ing lines and you have the recipe for a truly great story.

978-1-85078-797-6

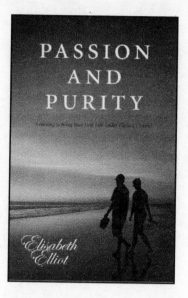

Passion and Purity

*Learning to Bring Your
Love Life Under Christ's
Control*

Elisabeth Elliot

Very few books have stood the test of time like *Passion and Purity*. Its much-needed message remains strong and hopeful in an age when doing whatever feels right is common practice. Using her own life as an example, Elisabeth Elliot guides singles of both genders and of any age on how to put their love lives under the authority of Jesus Christ. *Passion and Purity* covers dating issues such as: how to know which person is the right one to marry; loving passionately while remaining sexually pure; the man's and woman's role in relationships; putting God's desires ahead of personal desires; and how far is too far, physically.

978-1-85078-932-1

Authentic

We trust you enjoyed reading this book from Authentic Media. If you want to be informed of any new titles from this author and other exciting releases you can sign up to the Authentic newsletter online:

www.authenticmedia.co.uk

Contact us
By Post: Authentic Media
52 Presley Way
Crownhill
Milton Keynes
MK8 0ES

E-mail: info@authenticmedia.co.uk

Follow us: